ON EAST HILL

Life on the North Downs
recalled by Jack Hollands

Jack Hollands at his bungalow at East Hill, 1998.

ON EAST HILL
Life on the North Downs
recalled by Jack Hollands

Written and edited by
A.M. Parkin

Phillimore

2006

Published by
PHILLIMORE & CO. LTD
Shopwyke Manor Barn, Chichester, West Sussex, England
www.phillimore.co.uk

ISBN   1-86077-414-8
ISBN 13   978-1-86077-414-0

Printed and bound in Great Britain by
MPG BOOKS LTD
Bodmin, Cornwall

Cover illustration: Washing sheep at Spudgers Pond, 1903. Pasturing sheep was one of the ways the farmers on the North Downs scraped a living at the turn of the century. Along with their own small flocks, each year a thousand sheep from Romney Marsh were overwintered on the hills. Jack's father was a sheep drover at times.

The sheep were penned in with chestnut hurdles made in the woods and Hills Lane was blocked for the operation. The sheep were washed to bring up the wool prior to shearing.

Contents

List of Illustrations

Acknowledgements

My first acknowledgement is obviously to Jack for his patience over many visits. This book is his story and I have tried to convey it as faithfully as possible.

I should also like to thank Kent Archaeological Society, both for a grant from the Allen Grove Local History Fund which supported the publication of the first booklet in 1998, and for a further grant in 2006 which helped with this edition.

Peter Milner, son of the Rev. Robert Milner, Vicar of Woodlands from 1929-57, kindly supplied the memoir by Eliza Vincent describing the revival of the manor of Woodlands in the 19th century (see Appendix).

With this book I am chiefly grateful to Jack's niece, Susan Brazier, for access to Jack's archive and backing with the publication in tribute to Jack.

So often this kind of oral history is lost. It is encouraging to know that some people think it worth preserving.

I acknowledge with thanks the sources of the illustrations: A.M. Parkin, frontispiece and nos 1, 3, 8, 9, 16; Museum of English Rural Life, no. 5; all others from Jack Hollands' collection.

Monty Parkin, 2006

Preface

Following the publication of two oral history booklets on the village of Kemsing in 1990, I was given a few contacts at East Hill, on the hills above, in case I ever decided to do something similar there. Sadly, by the time I got round to following these up, most had gone and their memories with them.

Luckily, one very good contact survived in the form of Jack Hollands and, as soon as I started talking to him, I realised he had such a wealth of information that he would need a booklet to himself. This was published in 1998 and, to the surprise of both Jack and myself, quickly sold out.

After publication, other material came to light and I continued to visit Jack and make notes from our conversations. The intention was at some point to publish an expanded version. Sadly, Jack died in June 2005 whilst we were still discussing additional material.

Although I have added a brief historical background, this is not meant to be a comprehensive history of the area. For this I refer you to the bibliography.

This is the story of the Morgan and Hollands families, plus Jack's accumulated store of knowledge, most of it passed down in true oral history fashion.

Although the Morgan connection goes back here to at least the 18th century, Jack's narrative really begins in the late 19th century with the farmers and woodmen living and working close to the land, grateful for any small bonuses, such as wild rabbits, that the hilly terrain offered. Jack then charts the evolution of the area down to the 1990s.

Many people think of this stretch of downland as a remote and even mysterious place, so I hope Jack's story throws some light on it and brings its recent history to life.

Main Locations

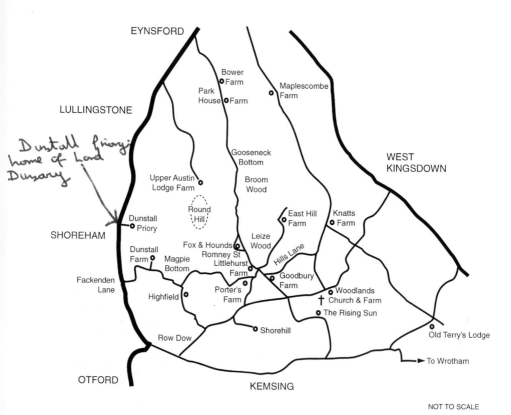

EYNSFORD

Bower Farm

Maplescombe Farm

Park House Farm

LULLINGSTONE

Gooseneck Bottom

WEST KINGSDOWN

Upper Austin Lodge Farm

Broom Wood

Round Hill

Dustall Priory home of Lord Dunsany

East Hill Farm

Knatts Farm

Dunstall Priory

SHOREHAM

Leize Wood

Fox & Hounds

Dunstall Farm

Magpie Bottom

Romney St Littlehurst Farm

Hills Lane

Goodbury Farm

Fackenden Lane

Porter's Farm

Highfield

Woodlands Church & Farm

The Rising Sun

Shorehill

Old Terry's Lodge

Row Dow

To Wrotham

OTFORD

KEMSING

NOT TO SCALE

On East Hill

Life on the North Downs
recalled by Jack Hollands

My family have lived on the hills for generations. They mostly worked on farms or in the woods, but a couple of them also ran the pub, so my family story gives quite a good picture of the way of life up here.

I was born in 1920 in the flint farm cottages at Tinkerpot Lane, Woodlands. The pair still stands on the bank just up from the church. At the time my father, Horace Hollands, was doing general farm work at Woodlands Farm for Sam Clark.

His father, another Horace Hollands, came to this area as a tenant farmer at Park House Farm, above Eynsford, in 1895. He later gave up the farm and kept the *Fox and Hounds* pub at Romney Street from 1904 till 1944. But on my mother's side, the Morgans, my connection with this area goes back much further. I can trace her line right back to John Groombridge, who was born in 1754. He married a local girl at Shoreham in 1772 and died in

1 Woodlands Farm cottages, where Jack was born in 1920. Jack's family lived on the right.

2 Edwin 'Tiny' Groombridge (1796-1896). Jack's great-great-grandfather was illiterate and worked on farms or in woods all his life. His one experience of rail travel gave him a panic attack.

1826. The fact that he's registered at Shoreham doesn't necessarily mean that he lived there, because people from up here used Shoreham Church before Woodlands Church was rebuilt on the hills in 1850. Groombridges have been around in this area for a very long time. In one of his drawings, the artist Samuel Palmer includes the Groombridges' house.[1]

I know nothing about John Groombridge but I do know a little about his son, Edwin Groombridge, who was born in 1796. Edwin is my great-great-grandfather on mother's side. Edwin was the youngest of about eight children. He never grew to be very tall so they nicknamed him 'Tiny'. He lived to be nearly a hundred. We're sure his dates are 1796-1896, despite the fact that in 19th-century census reports the figures given for his age are not consistent. Early reports have him older than later ones, as if he were growing younger! Censuses are obviously not that reliable. Tiny probably lost track himself of exactly how old he was.

He was baptised at Shoreham Church and was also married and buried there. People said, 'Why bury him at Shoreham?' because, by the time he died, Woodlands Church had been built and he attended there, but, after all, he was baptised and married at Shoreham so why not bury him there? His grave is not marked; the family were too poor to mark it. As with his father, John, because he's registered at Shoreham that doesn't mean he lived there. I think he lived most of his life at Romney Street, in a cottage that stood where the two bungalows are now. He was illiterate and probably worked on farms and in woodland all his life. That was all the work there was up here: farming and wooding.

We don't have much information on Tiny, but there is a story that has been passed down in the family. This concerns his one and only train journey.

Not long after the railway came to Shoreham in 1862, when Tiny was in his sixties, a couple of his daughters decided to take him on a train so that he could experience this new way of travelling. From Romney Street they walked down to Shoreham station. The girls then took him from Shoreham to Eynsford – only one stop, and I don't suppose the train went more than 30 m.p.h., but Tiny panicked and said the hedgerows were going by too fast and he couldn't get his breath. He was in a real state by the time they got off at Eynsford and said he'd never go on a train again. They all had to walk back home. Tiny preferred the simple life up on the hills.

One of Tiny's daughters, Elizabeth, was my grandfather's mother, though it isn't exactly straightforward. She had married a James Morgan in 1862 at Woodlands Church and borne him a daughter, but soon after that James died. Then, in 1868, when she was a widow, she had my grandfather Henry out of wedlock. He was given the name Morgan, despite the fact that his real father was known to be Henry Deamer, a local widower. To complicate things further, Elizabeth died in childbirth and so Henry Morgan, my grandfather, and Elizabeth's earlier child, Harriet, were brought up by their grandparents – poor old Tiny Groombridge and his wife Matilda, who had already brought up 12 children of their own. I said it wasn't straightforward.

3   Woodlands Church. The medieval church was abandoned but a new church was built by the Vincent family and consecrated in 1850. They added a small school next to it, which was attended by Henry Morgan and Bavo Booker.

It must have been very difficult for Tiny and Matilda taking on the two grandchildren, as by then they were both in their seventies. Being poor, they received a little help from the parish, which in the 1870s amounted to a shilling a week for each child and a loaf of bread for the family. In order to receive this, Matilda had to present the children each week at Shoreham vicarage, a five-mile walk there and back by the footpaths from Romney Street. A hard walk in all weathers for an elderly lady and two small children. No doubt Tiny supplemented their diet by catching wild rabbits, as everyone did up here. Matilda could boil them over the open fire, which was her only means of cooking in the Romney Street cottage. My mother said they were all still living on rabbits when she was young. There wasn't much meat going apart from that – rabbit pie, rabbit stew.

The only other memories we have of Tiny are from the 1890s, when he was very old. My mother, who was four when he died, said that he always wore a bowler hat, even indoors at the cottage in Romney Street. He would doze by the fire, hat on his head, sitting on a low wooden chair, the very basic sort that the 'bodgers' would make in the woods. He only needed a small chair because he was so tiny – they always called it 'the old chap's chair'. Well, one day, he nodded forward in his sleep and his bowler hat fell straight on the fire. But they managed to rescue it.[2] Mother's other memory was of accompanying him to Woodlands Church each Sunday, not long before he died in 1896. He would sit in the pew next to the donkey stove. Woodlands Church could be very cold, so Tiny always made sure he sat himself right next to that warm stove. As I said, he is buried in Shoreham churchyard in an unmarked grave.

So Henry Morgan, my grandfather, grew up at Romney Street in the care of Tiny and Matilda Groombridge, his grandparents. In the 1870s he went to the little school at Woodlands, next to the church. The Vincent family, who came here in the 1830s and rebuilt the church, also built the school. But Henry only went to school when he could afford the twopence a week it cost. He said he would have to go tying up bundles of wood faggots to earn a few coppers to pay for his schooling. I don't know if the school charged him for the door he split there. One day he was put outside for being naughty and he kicked the door so hard he split it.

When he left school in 1882, Henry went to work as a waggoner for George Booker, the son of Henry Booker, his neighbour at Romney Street. The Bookers were his landlords. Everyone knew George as 'Bavo' Booker. He

4   Henry Morgan and George 'Bavo' Booker at Gooseneck Bottom, 1890s. Bavo Booker was a hay and wood dealer. Jack's grandfather, Henry Morgan (left), went to work for Bavo as a waggoner aged 14, transporting hay and wood products to Dartford and outer London. The tarpaulin above the stack was used to protect it prior to thatching.

was a successful hay and wood dealer – there was a big trade in both up here, supplying towns to the north such as Dartford and into outer London. Bavo Booker had his head screwed on all right. He hadn't had much education – he went to the old Woodlands school like grandfather – but he knew how to get along. When grandfather wanted to buy his first suit, Bavo Booker went with him to the outfitters in Dartford. Bavo said to grandfather 'How much money you got?' but grandfather didn't want to tell him. Bavo said 'Well, have you got a sovereign?' and grandfather said 'Yes', so Bavo showed him how to bargain for a suit and knock the price down. He always knew how to get a good deal.

Bavo married a schoolmistress from Farningham. They originally lived in a big wooden caravan that he'd built, which was parked for years at Broom Wood on the road down to Eynsford. Bavo rented some hay fields in that area, at Gooseneck Bottom. He also took on Warren Farm, at the top of Fackenden Lane, where he made hay. They grew hay rather than wheat

5   Carting wood faggots. Bavo Booker did a round on the hills selling wood faggots for fire-lighting. Locally these were known as 'bavins', so he called out 'Bav, bavo, bavino' as he went, giving rise to his nickname. He also sold root vegetables and wild rabbits.

because the soil was so heavy to work. They used to enrich the hay crop by running a seed barrow over the fields to add some clover and so on. They didn't plough and sow the hay fields like they do now.

Grandfather used to have to take the loads of hay up to Dartford and beyond, so he was on the road quite a bit. He said he once got fined for falling asleep in charge of the waggon, which was an offence, you see. He said he was coming back from Dartford with an empty waggon, and it was a lovely sunny day, and as he got near Farningham he was sitting in the corner of the waggon and he must have nodded off. The next thing he knew a policeman had his hand on the reins and was saying to him 'You were asleep'. Grandfather said 'No, I wasn't,' but he had to go to Dartford court and was fined five shillings. You could also be fined for having no lights at night. They had big paraffin lamps that they had to hang on the waggons.

One of the places he delivered to in Dartford was Stricklands, the corn and hay dealers. The farmers up here only used to grow a little bit of corn or oats for horse feed, and if they had some left over they would sell it to Stricklands. They sold most of the hay crop, but obviously kept a bit back for their own animals. They had a saying about hay: 'Use half your hay by Candlemas Day' (2 February). In other words, if you managed to have half your hay left by the beginning of February you would be all right until the spring grass came.

To feed the horses, trusses of hay were cut up in a chaff-cutter. Oats and corn were also rolled, that's to say crushed, and the oats and chaff were mixed together for horse feed. 'Chaff' was also what they called the husks of corn left after threshing. That would be bagged up for the horses too. Some of the hay was cut later and, one year, when grandfather was helping with the haymaking, he and another worker decided to take a day off to go to Wrotham Hiring Fair. That was quite a big event where workers were still hired for a bit of money and a suit of clothes. But there was also some entertainment and drinking there. So grandfather and his mate had a good day out but the next day Bavo told them they could have another day off. He made them miss a day's work, and a day's pay, to teach them a lesson for missing work to go to the Hiring Fair.

Although hay was a very big trade – after all, horses provided all the transport so hay was the fuel, so to speak, like petrol today – and grandfather was kept busy with it, the trade in wood and wood products was even bigger. In fact there was more money made from the woods up here than there was from farming. Bavo Booker, aside from his hay business, would buy up cants of wood and employ a dozen men on piece work. A 'cant' was an area of coppice wood where the crop was the same age and ready for cutting. The coppice woods, mainly chestnut and hazel, were cut in rotation. All the rough wood went into faggots, or 'bavins' as we called them, used for lighting fires. There was a big demand for those. Bavo sold some of the cut wood locally from a horse and cart – on the hills and around the villages. He mostly sold bundles of faggots or, as I say, 'bavins', so he called out, 'Bav, bavo, bavino' as he went. This is what gave him the nickname 'Bavo' Booker. He would also call out 'Wild rabbits' because he sold those, too, along with eggs, butter, fruit and root vegetables. He would go round every week.

They took a lot of wood products northwards into London – the faggots for fire lighting and things like pea boughs and bean sticks for the garden. The garden stuff was mainly of hazel. To tie up a bundle of faggots, or any bundle, they would use 'whiffs', thin hazel twigs with an eye made in one end. The other end was twisted round the bundle and threaded through the eye and pulled tight. Some of the bundles of kindling would be made up by independent 'pimp makers'. A 'pimp' was another name for a bundle. They'd buy a cord (128 cubic feet) of cut wood from people like Bavo Booker and split it into kindling themselves. They originally tied them with whiffs, as I said, but later they had pimping machines to tie the bundles. The machines would pull the wire or string up tight round the bundle.

Quite a lot of rough faggots went for haystack bottoms. The farmers would build their stacks on a layer of faggots. They also made thatching splints out of hazel. The thatch used to be held on by long sticks held down by splints, bent like a staple. The hazel was also split and woven into fence panels known as wattle hurdles. Because these were closely woven they gave some protection from the weather. The wattle hurdles sheltered newborn lambs, for instance, from the cold winds. Wattle is also a very old building material. When it was smeared with a mixture of clay, dung and animal hair, it made 'wattle and daub', which you find in old buildings.

And of course they produced loads of hop poles made from the chestnut. Chestnut was the other coppice wood. There was still a big demand for hop poles in the days when they picked the hops directly from the poles, rather than strings. They'd make fencing and hurdles from the chestnut as well. The woodman would set up what was known as a 'brake' to hold the wood while he split it. Chestnut splits very nicely and split wood, which follows the grain, is stronger than sawn wood. Split chestnut poles were called 'spiles' or stakes. He'd split it with a dull axe. The bark was taken off with a round blade with a wooden handle. Then he'd make it up into gate hurdles which you would use to pen your sheep in. You could move chestnut hurdles around to fold your sheep on some turnips or pen them in when they were being washed – as in the picture of Spudgers Pond. They even produced a kind of short bean stick that was used for ships' fenders. Sticks were used before they had rubber. In fact, during the Second World War they went back to using sticks.

Then there were besoms made from birch; the gardeners used those for sweeping up the leaves. It was the twigs that were used for the brush. Grandfather Henry was a dab hand at making those. They used to bring him a 'kit' of birch, a large bundle, and he would fashion the broom and pull it up tight with straps, then bind it with wire or split cane. Then he'd push in a pointed handle and the thing was made. He'd do bundles of them

– gardeners would buy half a dozen at a time. Of course the police also used sticks of birch in those days to birch boys in the police station. They used to soak the birch before hitting them with it. If you get a birch twig that's been wetted that doesn't half give you a wipe. Six strokes would be very painful. That was a common punishment for scrumping or things like that. The police truncheons were made from ash.

All in all, they grew wood for every purpose up here. There was a lot of ash grown which was used to make waggons – ash was light for the body. They made Sussex waggons around this area, they were different to what they called the 'Devon waggon', which was shaped in front like a boat. There were different kinds of carts made as well. Apart from the ordinary tip carts, there were Norfolk and Scotch carts. The Scotch carts were two-wheeled and bigger than the usual ones. They said the Scottish farmers brought those down when a lot of them migrated south to take over farms. And, of course, all the brewers had coopers who made their barrels for them, so oaks were grown for those. The wood had to be seasoned out for the barrels. The oak bark would be stripped off for use in tanning hides. A tannery was found near Broughton in Otford. It had pipes made from hollowed out beech.

They had sawpits up here to rough-cut the bigger trunks. The trunks would be hauled up on to a timber tug, an open waggon, by horses. It was done quite slowly – they'd move the trunk up a foot at a time. Grandfather said the horses got very good at it. They understood the procedure and seemed to know what manoeuvre was needed. The trunks were tied on with metal chains. Then they would haul the loaded timber tugs over to the sawpits. There, one man stood at the top and another in the pit and they'd saw up the trunks with great long saws. Those saws must have been good. They'd cut the wood into rough planks. Grandfather said the man at the top had to guide the saw but the poor chap at the bottom got showered with sawdust all day. The trunks were held in place by metal 'dogs', so the man underneath was known as the 'underdog'. There seems to have been a sawpit next to the road in Leize Wood near here. I suppose they would have had it by the road to make it easier for transporting the wood away.

They also used to get charcoal burners in Leize Wood who came and lived on the site. They came up until the First World War. Before the blacksmiths got coke they would have used charcoal. It was still used in various industries and the hops were dried in the hop kilns using charcoal. There was still a big demand for it. The charcoal burners would tackle a piece of Leize Wood every year. They'd live in a caravan or build a rough shelter. Father said they were a dirty old crowd. They would build their big round stack out of lengths of cord wood, thickish poles about four foot long. A 'cord' of wood was a heap of it made between stakes, four feet wide, four feet high and eight feet long, giving 128 cubic feet. They'd cover the stack with straw and dirt and ashes from previous fires. They'd 'dirt it all in' as they said. Then they'd take out a pole from the middle and light it from there with burning charcoal. They had to stay on hand to keep an eye on it so it didn't burst into flame and reduce the lot to ashes. The wood had to be slowly charred over several days. As I said, we never saw them up here after the First World War so the demand for charcoal must have been dying off.

The cutting of the wood would all be done in winter. Come October, when the leaves began to fall, men like Bavo's piece workers would start cutting. Then they'd carry on until spring. They weren't allowed to cut after 21 March. Towards the end of the cutting season they would go what they called 'splashing'. They'd cut a lot of wood down in a rush so they could make it up later. Even in my time, in the 1920s, I used to hear them say 'We've got to go splashing now so we've got a job for another month or two'. When the cutting was finished they could then go back over what they'd 'splashed' and spend a month or six weeks making it up. They'd cut up the wood and turn it into whatever was wanted – pea boughs, bean poles, stuff for the garden. Or they'd split up the bigger bits for fencing and hurdles and use up all the rough wood for bundles of faggots. A record of how much they'd earned was kept on notched tally sticks – so even the accounts were done with wood.

Then they'd have to go haymaking or do other seasonal work. There was a certain amount of root crops grown up here – turnips, swedes and potatoes – so there'd be hoeing work. The farming was very labour intensive. I can remember lots of men working up here, and of course there were even more in grandfather's time. There would be big families living in the cottages, and lots of people sharing a few rooms. The farmers would house workers in the farmhouse – many workers lived on the farms and the farmer fed them. Casual workers often slept in barns or outhouses. They would sleep in straw – even in the 1930s some children in farm cottages still slept in straw.

When my mother was a little girl and grandfather Morgan was living at Goodbury Farm, a man and his wife, who were doing hoeing work, slept in the chaff house. That was part of the stable – the chaff was the horses' feed, as I've mentioned. The stable had a door opening on to the grassy bank at the side of Goodbury Road. Early one morning the man came to my grandmother and said his wife was ill. In fact my grandmother could see at once that the woman was having a baby. Someone went for Dr Dupré, the doctor at Shoreham, and he came up on his hunter horse. He'd always jump a hedge or two if he was in a hurry. Dr Dupré rolled up his shirtsleeves to attend the woman and my mother was told to keep the fire going to provide him with hot water. As the chaff house was so cramped, the woman eventually had her baby, a little girl, on the grassy bank at the side of the road. Mother and baby were later taken back to their home in Dartford by pony cart.

A lot of Bavo Booker's men would sleep in barns. One of the things he fed them on was a dish of bread and milk, because there was plenty of both up here. Mrs Booker would break up the bread in a pot and pour milk over it and boil it, so the bread was scalded. She'd give that to the men. She sometimes used to give it to grandfather Morgan when he was working for Bavo, even though he had a home to go to. We used to eat bread and milk ourselves as children, and I still occasionally eat it for breakfast to this day.

Grandfather Morgan only stopped working for Bavo Booker because of the First World War. Bavo wanted to keep his son Sid out of the army, so he sacked grandfather in order to claim he didn't have any men for the haymaking and wood-cutting, and needed his son. Haymaking was very important, because transport was still nearly all horses and they had to be fed, so you could be kept at home if you were in such an essential job. In fact the army could commandeer haystacks and horses if they wanted them. So anyway, Bavo sacked grandfather and said he needed his son Sid.

As it happens, Bavo's plan didn't work, because Sid was later called up anyway, when the war situation worsened. Be that as it may, around 1915 grandfather Henry left Bavo and went to work for Lord Dunsany at Dunstall, where he became the wood reeve. He was still living in the cottage in Romney Street which belonged to Bavo. So, after sacking him Bavo wrote him a letter saying he should charge grandfather rent now. At Dunstall, grandfather Morgan looked after all the woodland. There was a great deal of it covering the hills. Of course he had learned about wooding through his work with Bavo. He supervised the planting and cutting and maintained the fences around the boundaries. He also kept the rideways clear for shooters, because there was game in the woods.

I suppose you'd call the whole area hunting and shooting territory – even the pub's called the *Fox and Hounds*. The Sugdens, who owned the Kingsdown estate, would bring shooting parties over to East Hill. They'd meet at East Hill farm for lunch. Two old ladies, Betsy Baker and her sister, lived at the farm and did the catering. They kept chickens and grandfather Morgan used to deliver chicken corn to them. And the West Kent Hunt used to meet at Highfield when the Cohens were there. The West Kent Hunt came through the woods regularly. There were some hunting gates at the wood entrances, little five-bar gates with a weight that swung open and back as the horses went through.

Grandfather was quite keen on horses. He used to go each year to the horse racing at the old Greatness racetrack. He said it was a really big affair – people came in carriages and brakes from all around. He said once when he went there he got into a fight and his eye was black for a week.

Lord Dunsany had lots of chestnut plantations and, as the trees died, grandfather would plant another, or if there was a space he would fill it. Chestnut was the main crop they wanted there. But he also planted oaks and beeches, which would be left standing a long time while the other wood was cut. He would plant eight oaks or beeches to the acre, with quicker crops around them.

They used to sell off cants of wood to dealers like Bavo. Henry would have to see that they cleared up properly. The wood-cutters were supposed to clear up when they had finished, but they were always in a hurry, and what they didn't want they would just throw to one side. As wood reeve, grandfather had to make sure they left things tidy.

When he was working in the woods, he would set up a rough shelter by banging four hazel stakes in the ground and covering them with tarpaulin. That's where he would go for a smoke or a bite to eat – he would have a fire in there to make tea. He usually wore felt or moleskin wrapped round the bottom of his trousers – you can see that in the old photograph (illustration 6).

Grandfather worked under Lord Dunsany's head gardener, Wilson, at Dunstall. Grandfather didn't have much to do with Lord Dunsany directly. Dunsany was away with his regiment in the First World War. He didn't live at Dunstall Priory permanently until after the war, when he settled there to write.[3]

Grandfather said that no one was allowed to go past the front of the house, Dunstall Priory, until after 11 a.m. Perhaps Lord Dunsany was up half the night writing. Later, Lord Dunsany had a hut in the woods off Fackenden Lane where he could go to write. It was along a path below

Dunstall Farm. No one was allowed in the woods when he was there. Grandfather went past the hut one day, thinking the coast was clear, but then realised Lord Dunsany was in the hut. Dunsany spotted him. He didn't say anything directly, but the next day Wilson, the head gardener, said to grandfather 'You didn't half get me into trouble yesterday!' Still, people had a safe job working for Lord Dunsany, and in fact grandfather Morgan was still cutting wood for the gardens at Dunstall – pea boughs and bean sticks – when he was over eighty. It was in the woods up Fackenden Lane where he did his last bit of cutting. He died in 1961 when he was 93.

I haven't said much about grandmother Morgan. She was originally Elizabeth Hoad and she and grandfather were married in 1889. They had eight children, the first, Lizzie, being born before they were married. Elizabeth had already had another daughter, Minnie Hoad, by someone else before she was married. It's a complicated family tree, isn't it?

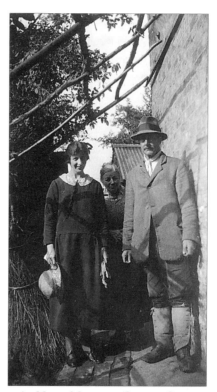

6 Henry Morgan at Romney Street, *c.*1916, with his wife, Elizabeth and daughter, Nellie. After bring sacked by Bavo Booker at the beginning of the First World War, Henry became wood reeve for Lord Dunsany. When working in the woods, he wore felt or moleskin around his trousers to keep out the damp.

Henry and grandmother Morgan lived mainly in one of a pair of cottages in Romney Street, next to the *Fox and Hounds* pub. The cottages are still there – they were actually built by Bavo Booker. Before Henry and Elizabeth moved in, a gamekeeper called John Daniels, who everyone knew as 'Old Daniels', had lived there. Old Daniels had once been the keeper on the Woodlands estate but he'd got the sack for some mysterious reason, no one knew what. When he lived in Romney Street he spent all his time in the *Fox and Hounds* which, as I said, was next door, so quite a handy local for him. But one day, after drinking in the *Fox and Hounds*, he went back to the cottage next door and shot himself. No one knows why. So the cottage became empty, and because Old Daniels had shot himself there, nobody wanted it. But Henry Morgan hadn't long been married and he needed somewhere, so he took it. He wasn't so fussy. Eventually, of course, the son of Horace Hollands from the *Fox and Hounds* married the daughter of Henry Morgan from the cottage next door and that's how the two families came together.

Grandmother Morgan had a tough time bringing up all those children because there wasn't a lot of money around. Although the kids didn't starve, my mother said gran wasn't a very good cook. She used to just boil everything and make stews – especially rabbit stew. The wild rabbits up here were still just as important a part of people's diet as they had been in Tiny Groombridge's day. I suppose it wasn't easy for gran, not having a stove or kitchen range – she had to cook everything in a pot over an open fire. Some cottages had a pothook hanging down from the chimney, but she could only rest the pots on a bar over the open fire.

This meant the fire was very important, both for heating and cooking. So they would like to have everything ready to get the fire going in the morning. You would hear people late at night chopping up sticks for the fire, which they would need to boil the pot for their morning tea – they started work very early. They liked to have kindling wood ready but you would hear them cursing in the morning if the wood was damp and they couldn't get the fire started.

Grandmother used to buy flour directly from Mr Norton, the miller, who had the windmill at Kingsdown. She would buy plain flour and put baking powder or whatever in it. Mr Norton came round on a horse and cart selling flour and 'middlings' (pig feed) and other stuff. When they grind the wheat, the wheat germ makes the flour and the coarse outer casing is called 'middlings' – that's what made the pig feed. The pig feed he sold was mainly for the farmers, but some people kept their own pigs. Grandfather had a couple of pigsties at the bottom of the garden, and there were two or three sties at the *Fox and Hounds*.

The *Fox and Hounds* also had a bread oven built in to the wall of the taproom. There was another bread oven at the *Rising Sun* – pubs often baked bread because, in the days when they brewed their own beer, they had the yeast anyway for that. Mr Farley, who is in the picture of the 1897 jubilee (illustration 7), was the last baker at the *Fox and Hounds*. The brick

7   Queen Victoria's Diamond Jubilee, 1897. For the Jubilee a group photograph was
taken of most of the residents of East Hill, Romney Street and Woodlands.
    In this section are Frank Farley (top right), the last publican to bake bread at the *Fox
and Hounds*, John Daniels (top row, second from left), the gamekeeper who shot himself
in the cottage next to the *Fox and Hounds*, and the Rev. John Handcock (third row down,
with two children on his knee), the vicar of Woodlands from 1860-1907.

oven was heated with wood faggots, then the ashes raked out when it was
hot enough. When Mr Farley baked he worked a long day and it was a
very hot job. Naturally, as the oven was in the taproom, he would have a
drink while he was working. So he would bake some bread and get a bit
hot and have a beer and bake some more bread and get a bit hotter and
have some more beer and mother said he would always finish up drunk
on baking day. Sometimes the children would play tricks on him – once
they threw sand in the flour and everybody had gritty bread. People were
probably relieved when he gave up and a baker from Shoreham started
doing a round on the hills.
    The *Fox and Hounds* also ran a shop where they sold dry goods – tea,
sugar, currants, sweets and so on, anything that kept. A grocer from Shoreham,

Lovelands, also came up here with a horse and van. Then there was Mr Kipps, the butcher from Otford. He couldn't have sold much, because he came up on horseback carrying all the meat in a wicker basket. I suppose a basketful was all he needed for the trade he would do. By coming on horseback he could use the bridleways and take shortcuts.

Horses continued to be used for a long time up here, even after the Second World War. In my day I can remember Bob Groves, another butcher from Otford, coming up in the 1920s on a box trap pulled by a pony. He sat high up to the rear and there was a door in the back of the box which he opened to get the meat. But people couldn't afford much butcher's meat. If they bought a bob's worth of 'pudding meat', pudding steak, they thought that was good.

To keep their meat people had meat safes against the north wall of the house. These were boxes with metal gauze over them. As soon as they bought their meat from the butcher it went straight into the meat safe. Sometimes, in really hot weather, they'd put it in a box down a well. There might be a well reserved especially for the purpose. They'd lower a box with the meat and the milk down the well to keep it cool. Of course the milk originally came fresh from the cow so it would go off very quickly. They'd often scald the milk to make it keep – not boil it.

Generally grandmother stayed at home looking after the house and children, but she would sometimes go out and do seasonal work. She often took the children with her. In the early part of the century, my mother can remember going out stone picking with grandmother. They would go to the big field at Goodbury Farm. They'd pick the stones off after it had been ploughed ready for autumn sowing. These fields were full of flints, as fast as they picked them off the top, more would come up – people used to say the stones 'grew'. Lots of mothers went with their children, although some men did it too. The pickers would collect the stones in buckets and have to fill up a wooden 'yard' box, a bottomless frame about two feet high, which held a square yard. They were paid so much a yard, but it wasn't much. Then the stones would be put on a tip cart and they'd shoot them out at different spots along the road so the roadman could use them. There did used to be a belief that picking stones off the fields helped produce better crops, but it made little difference. The farmers up here mainly did it to sell the stones to the council to make a bit of money. The council bought stones from the farmers for making up the roads.

The roadman, or 'lengthsman' would knap the flints to keep the road surface good; my mother used to watch them doing that. She remembered 'Old Rooter', the lengthsman, breaking up stones with a round hammer. He sometimes wore goggles with a fine wire mesh that would protect his eyes. Another lengthsman she remembered later was 'Kenty', who'd been a soldier in the First World War. She said you couldn't help noticing that at Christmas time Kenty would always find a job to do near Highfield, the big house of Sir Herbert Cohen, because Sir Herbert would give him a Christmas box. In Kenty's time they would tar the roads using a boiler on a cart to heat the tar. From a tap they ran it into water cans, poured it on the road and chucked sand on it. The men got covered in tar. Kenty used to throw a few knobs of coal from the boiler over the hedge for himself. But he'd forget to collect them and they'd be picked up by farm workers weeks later. They'd say 'Here's some of Kenty's coal'. As well as keeping his stretch of road in good repair, the lengthsman had to keep it clean and cut back the hedges. He was responsible for a certain length of road.

Grandmother also used to go hop-picking at Maplescombe in the hop garden around the tiny flint church, or what remained of it.[4] Mother went hop-picking there with her, to earn money to pay for her boots for school. While they were hop-picking, grandmother would tell her stories of life on the hills, especially of the smugglers in the early 19th century who came up this way from Wrotham on their way to London with things like tea, brandy, lace and tobacco brought from the coast. There were various holes and tunnels up here where the smugglers hid their goods. At the bottom of my garden here, in East Hill Road, there used to be a tunnel which may have been a smugglers' hiding place. Over the years it has collapsed and filled in. There were many so-called 'dene holes' on the hills. Some of them were dug as chalk wells when they used to use the chalk for dressing fields. Some were flint mines. Others – we don't know what they were. There was a hole at Dunstall Farm that was very deep – I used to throw stones down it and they would bounce several times. That one's been filled in. So there were plenty of places to hide these goods, be they spirits or tobacco or whatever. They reckon the rock shelters at Oldbury Hill were used to hide contraband.

Some of the smugglers were based at Wrotham Heath. Old Terry's Lodge, to the east, which looks out from the hills over the valley to Wrotham, was one of the lookout posts. The farmer at Old Terry's Lodge, who was in with the smugglers, had two ways of signalling to them. At night he placed oil

8 'Smugglers' Cottage', Magpie Bottom. Jack's grandmother said this flint cottage beside the road was a smugglers' lookout post. On the hill in the background was the *Pig and Whistle* pub.

lamps in various windows and by day he kept different combinations of horses and cows tethered on the hillside, like a sort of semaphore. By checking the signals, the smugglers in the valley below could see if it was safe to come over the hills. There are quite a few records of clashes between the smugglers and the excise men in this area, especially at Shoreham. It was quite a dangerous business. It's said that one of the king's men captured at Shoreham in the 18th century was later found drowned on the beach at Lydd. He'd been pegged to the beach at low water and drowned by the incoming tide.

And some charcoal burners and small farmers in this area died much richer than they should have been. They left more money than they could have earned from their proper trades, so they were probably in league with the smugglers. The farmers could help the smugglers in various ways, apart from keeping lookout. If the smugglers used waggons, for instance, the farmers could drive their sheep over the tracks so it was impossible to see where they'd been.

Mother was told that the small cottage at Magpie Bottom, the flint one with its end wall next to the road, was another smugglers' lookout post.

There's a high wooden fence beside it, but if you peep through the fence on the western side you can see a green bottle sticking out of the wall. That's supposed to be a 'brandy slide', where the smugglers would pay the lookout by dropping a bottle in the hole, because the smugglers never liked to be seen. You could reach it as you were riding by. The person in the cottage would signal to them with a lamp in the window on the other side, the one that's now bricked up. That brandy slide hole may also have been a spy hole looking up towards a beer house that stood on the hill to the west. This beer house was called the *Pig and Whistle*, which some people said was a twist on 'peek and whistle'.[5] I suppose they thought that was how the lookout might signal to the smugglers. You can still see the remains of the *Pig and Whistle* in the wood to the west. There are bits of flint wall near the footpath amongst the trees. And not too far away in the same wood is a really good dene hole, probably a chalk well, which goes down beside a tree and opens out into three large caverns. That would have been a very good hiding place. I suppose this area, with all its remote byways, provided a good route into the Crays and Dartford and London for the smugglers. The *Pig and Whistle* would have been outside the territory of the Bow Street Runners.

9 Remains of the *Pig and Whistle*. Just a few pieces of flint wall remain in the wood across from the cottage. Because of its smuggling connection, the locals thought the name was a twist on 'peek and whistle' but the likely derivation is 'piggen wassail'.

If you really know the area it's surprising how you can get about. In my mother's day, a gypsy called Billy Howard used to pick primroses at Magpie Bottom, bunch them up and walk into Dartford to sell them. Billy always said he walked *straight* to Dartford – the most direct route, going under hedges or whatever. He could get there really quickly. Billy would pick anything growing wild that he could sell. He also picked other flowers, like violets or cowslips. And, later in the year, he gathered blackberries and mushrooms. In fact he was known as 'Blackberry Billy'. At Christmas time he would cut holly and make up wreaths. Once, when I was a boy, he stopped the school bus and asked the driver to give a wicker basket to Mr Pinkerton in the shop at Eynsford. It was full of mushrooms covered in cabbage leaves.

Billy never did any regular work. It was anything he could think of to get by. He might do a bit of hedge cutting or make up some pea boughs or bean sticks. And he would catch a few rabbits using wire snares. Sometimes he could catch them by hand or foot. He knew they would often hide in a patch of long grass in a field where a cowpat had been the previous year. So he'd creep up to the patch of grass and make a grab or just step on them. Sometimes if he was desperate he would sell bootlaces in Dartford. But he always seemed to manage to pay his way. He rented a wooden bungalow from one of the farmers. He got a pension eventually and, when he collected it from the post office at Goodbury, he would have to make his mark, he couldn't write. Some of the other old boys had no pensions or anything. They would keep going in their seventies and eighties doing a bit of hedge-cutting or anything to stay alive. But some would eventually finish up in the workhouse at Sundridge. One day, while hedge-cutting, Billy cut his finger really badly and mother bandaged it for him. Although he had a crooked finger ever afterwards, he was always grateful to her for doing it. He would wave his hand with the crooked finger to her.

All the Morgan children went to school at Kemsing – quite a walk down off the hills and back again. One of the daughters, Emma, died from diphtheria in 1904, aged seven. This was the disease that most commonly killed children. My mother said that Emma may have died because they couldn't afford to fetch a doctor – you had to pay for the doctor then. There seemed to be an outbreak of diphtheria every few years. Mother thought some diseases might have been spread by such things as a dirty bucket in the well at Kemsing. She certainly thought the sanitation arrangements at Kemsing school could have caused the outbreak that killed Emma. Piped water was only laid on to the school in the early 1900s, while mother was there. Before that there had just been buckets to supply the water and for use as toilets. After piped water arrived and the school acquired flush toilets, the boys thought it was a great game to keep flushing the loos. In the end the headmaster, Mr Jordan, forbade the children to flush them and said he would go round from time to time and flush them all himself. That doesn't sound too healthy either, does it?

Mother and her brothers and sisters walked down to Kemsing school with the other children from up here – the Clarks from Woodlands and the Bookers from Cotman's Ash. That was a nice walk down off the hills in summer but not so good in winter. When it was really foggy they would get lost – sometimes people had to go looking for them. On snowy days the children who'd had to walk a long way, from here or from Drane Farm, would be given a cup of hot cocoa in School House. That was provided by the church. Some of the children might have been glad of that because they might not have any lunch. There was one family up here that was so poor the children sometimes had nothing to take for their lunch break at school. Because they were ashamed to say they had nothing, they would say they were going home to eat and just go and stand on the hills till lunch hour was over. It wasn't unknown in the local schools for children to just faint in class because they were so undernourished.

In the winter the 'hill children', as they were called, were let out early so they could get home before dark. Sometimes the old vicar of Woodlands, the Rev. John Handcock, would visit the school and ask all 'his' children in the class to stand, meaning the hill children. Mother thought very highly of 'Mr Handcock', as she called him, and talked a lot about him. He was Irish and the vicar of Woodlands for 47 years, from 1860 until 1907, when he died aged seventy-eight. When he first moved into the vicarage up here his wife brought some of her family from Ireland with her, including her younger brother, whose name was Hyacinth. You can't help wondering what the locals – those rough wood-cutters and the like – made of a boy called Hyacinth living at the vicarage. Mr Handcock's first wife died but he remarried in the 1870s. His new wife had always lived in a town and she was quite shocked at how isolated it was at Woodlands. In fact one day she said to her charlady, 'It's very remote up here, what on earth do you do when you need a doctor?' and her charlady replied, 'Oh we don't trouble about no doctors in these parts ma'm, we mostly die natural deaths.'

Around the turn of the century Mr Handcock was in his seventies. He was especially fond of children, and, because of his encouragement, all the Morgan children attended church at Woodlands and were confirmed. Mother remembered being taken to Otford Church for confirmation by pony and cart, and having to walk back with the other children because the adults took all the space on the cart for the return journey. Her Aunt Harriet, from Crockenhill, brought all her children to be baptised at Woodlands Church because of Mr Handcock – they walked all the way there and back.

He cared about the sick and needy. He would take the church collection round to the poor and give produce to the sick. When Mr Handcock went visiting in his governess cart, he always wanted a couple of children to accompany him, to hold the pony while he made his calls. Although mother and the other children liked him, they thought that was a boring job, so when they heard him approaching their cottage at Goodbury Farm they'd say, "Ark, 'ere comes old 'Andcock' and they'd run and hide in the barn. But two of them would have to go. They ran errands for Mr Handcock. They'd go down to Otford station and collect his London newspapers from Mr Willis, the station master. They would also take Mr Handcock's watch to Mr Willis to be set by 'station time'. That was the only way of getting the right time before radio came in. Every morning Mr Willis would get a telegraph signal from London giving him the right time. He would set the station clock by that. Then Mr Handcock's watch would be set according to the station clock and the clocks at the vicarage would be set by his watch. So the church bell for services would always be rung at the right time and anyone setting their pocket watch by the church bell would know it was pretty accurate. Time was quite well synchronised really. The children would also help deliver things like fruit or bottles of wine to the sick. On one occasion mum's brother, Harry, had to go to the doctor at Farningham to collect a prescription for Mr Handcock. It was raining, and by the time Harry got home he was soaked. Mr Handcock paid for a new pair of boots for him. He would reward the girls too, with boiled sweets from a jar in his study, or a piece of 'bought' cake. Once he took them to the drapers at Bat and Ball and bought some material for their mother to make them new dresses.

Mr Handcock loved roses and, if he had an important visitor to the church, such as Sir Mark Collet from St Clere, he would take them round his rose garden. To help him in the garden he sometimes employed a man known as 'Old Oxford', who slept rough. Benjamin Harrison, from Ightham, famous for finding all sorts of prehistoric stone tools on these hills, would call in at the vicarage when he was on one of his expeditions on the Downs, or sometimes he'd come to Woodlands church on Sunday and stay for cakes and wine with Mr Handcock afterwards.[6] Because he was so kind, and cared for all the community, mother always said 'There was no-one like Mr Handcock'. He's buried in Woodlands Churchyard but the grave looks a bit neglected now.

One of mother's brothers, my uncle Henry James Morgan, the young 'Harry' I've just mentioned, was killed in the First World War. He was a couple of years younger than mother, having been born in 1894. Harry went with the others to Kemsing School, then worked in the gardens at Highfield for the Cohen family. I think Harry lodged in the

10   Harry Morgan, Jack's uncle. Son of Henry Morgan, Harry was involved in heavy fighting on the Western Front from 1915. He was injured a week before the Armistice and died three days after it.

gardeners' bothy there, because that's where apprentice boys usually lived. Then he got a job at the royal gardens at Windsor; a lot of men worked there. He left Windsor to work for a famous orchid grower, Sir William Herbert St Quintin, at Scampston Hall in Yorkshire.

Harry was a territorial soldier and he joined his Royal Artillery unit soon after war was declared in 1914. He went to France in 1915 and was on the Western Front right through the war. I think he only came home on leave twice. At the end of one leave, mother can remember him sitting by the fire in 'the old chap's chair', that rough wooden chair that belonged to Tiny Groombridge. The family kept that chair for years, and she remembered Harry sitting in it and saying he didn't want to go back, but of course he had to. He was at the Third Battle of Ypres in late 1917 with a howitzer battery. Then he was near Cambrai, where there was some heavy fighting. His luck finally ran out on 4 November 1918, just before the war ended. There was a mustard gas attack on the regiment's billet near Cambrai and he was gassed, wounded and burned while trying to help a friend. Harry had terrible injuries. He was sent to the base hospital at Rouen, but died on 14 November 1918, just three days after the Armistice had been signed. Back up on the hills at Romney Street, when they heard about the Armistice, Harry's younger brother Wally said 'Let's put out the flags to welcome Harry home', but grandmother Morgan said 'No, let's wait to see that he's safe first'. Shortly afterwards they learned that Harry had died just after the Armistice. He's buried at St Sever cemetery, south of Rouen.

Funnily enough, there was an artist living in Shoreham who did some propaganda for the First World War. That was Harold Copping and he used local people quite a lot as models for his work. One of the people he drew was Violet Clark, who later married Wally Morgan, Harry's younger brother, the one who'd said 'Let's put out the flags.'

Father said that during the First World War, if the wind was in the right direction, you could hear the guns from France up here night and day. There were defensive trenches dug across the hills, which were the last line of defence around London. There were three lines of trenches, with barbed wire entanglements in front. They came from beyond the *Rising Sun* in the east, ran above Shorehill, and on to Otford Mount going west. Soldiers were brought down to Otford station and marched up here to dig them. Oliver Lyle, who later built Shorehill, was an officer in charge of the men digging the trenches. Above Shorehill, the trenches crossed a field which was on the children's path to school at Kemsing. Boards were placed over the trenches, and a gap cut in the wire, so they could get through. But one evening Wally, just mentioned, worked late at school doing some gardening, and by the time he got back up on the hill it was dark and he couldn't find the gap in the wire. He panicked because he thought he'd be stranded on the hills all night and he ran up and down trying to find the gap and snagging himself on the barbed wire. But he got home eventually.

When I worked at Shorehill in the 1930s I could still see where the trenches had been. They were only roughly filled in afterwards. All they did was throw the barbed wire in the bottom of a trench and chuck some loose earth in. West of Shorehill, they ran across that field beside the top of Row Dow. The last time I walked over that field, going towards Otford Mount, I could still make out a slight depression about halfway across where one of the trenches had been, running roughly east to west towards a gate on the Otford side. I don't know how far the trenches went – I assume they made a great arc all the way up to the Thames.

It was during the First World War that uncle Wally got diphtheria, like aunt Emma before him. Wally was sent to the fever hospital at Wickham Field, on the outskirts of Otford. It was behind big double gates. The matron and the nurses lived in the house and behind it were two blocks, one for diphtheria and one for scarlet fever. You were kept in isolation – visitors couldn't get close to you. When grandmother Morgan visited Wally on a Sunday she had to just look at him through a window. If local children came walking by the hedge, the nurses checked to see if you had spoken to them. Any letters the patients sent home were baked in the oven. There were some soldiers

11   Horace Hollands, Jack's paternal grandfather, who ran the *Fox and Hounds* pub from 1904-44.

there, too, and their mates used to throw bars of chocolate over the wall. The soldiers would give them to Wally. Not everyone recovered, but Wally did, and before he came home they 'cooked' his clothes. A man called Mr Baker, as it happens, baked the clothes in the oven in the same way they baked your letters. Any toys you'd taken in you had to leave there. This was quite upsetting for some children if they'd taken their favourite toy in. Before you came home they would give you a bath and wash you with disinfectant. And they would fumigate the house before you moved back in. The family had to get out while they did it.

Another of mother's brothers, Arthur Morgan, known as 'Chummy', born in 1900, had the *Fox and Hounds* pub in Romney Street until 1961. But talking of the *Fox and Hounds*, I'd better get on to my father's side of the family, because my paternal grandfather, Horace Hollands, had the pub before Arthur, from 1904 until 1944.

I mentioned at the very beginning that grandfather Horace Hollands came up this way about 1895 to run Park House Farm in Bower Lane, above Eynsford. As with mother's side of the family, I can trace father's line back to the 18th century. Only whereas mother's side all came from this

12   The *Fox and Hounds*, Romney Street. Grandfather Horace ran it and grandfather Henry Morgan lived in the cottage next door to the right. Before the First World War the 'rough woodcutters' would be on the doorstep at 6 a.m. demanding a drink. There was a grindstone at the back where they could sharpen their axes.

area, the Hollandses mostly lived in Cowden, where they were millers. John Hollands, who lived from 1729 to 1811, was tenant of the Old Mill, Cowden, and his son Henry was the miller at Furnace Mill there. James Hollands, Henry's son and my great-great-grandfather, also had Furnace Mill, but his son Charles, who lived there from 1846-1930, moved to Wittersham and bought a farm. Grandfather Horace Hollands, born in 1867, was the second son of Charles and he started out as a miller. I think he worked at Burfoot Mill in Westerham and he also worked at mills in Greenwich. Soon after he married Ellen Lawrence in 1891, they went to live in Liverpool, where again he worked in mills. My father, another Horace Hollands, was born in Liverpool in 1892, but it wasn't long after that that grandfather Horace came to Eynsford to become the sub-tenant of Park House Farm. He had seen it advertised in *Hare and Hound*. Park House Farm is just above Bower Farm; they used to be separate, but I think they're all integrated now. They used to be part of the Lullingstone estate. The family lived in a farm cottage by the barn, not in the farm house.

Grandfather Horace didn't make much out of Park House Farm, it was just subsistence farming. So when the tenancy of the *Fox and Hounds* pub came up in 1904, he went in there as landlord and stayed for 40 years. My father was a boy of 12 when they took the pub. He was attending Eynsford School at the time and he carried on going there from the pub in Romney Street – quite a walk down Bower Lane. The brewers who leased the *Fox and Hounds*, Kidd's of Dartford, had given the previous tenants notice after a pretty short time because they couldn't control the customers. There were a lot of rough wood-cutters about. They would get drunk and start scrapping and the landlord couldn't control them. I think there had been a few court cases and the brewers didn't like it – the pub had got a reputation for trouble. One man got a heavy fine for smashing the door down. He'd been thrown out of the pub five times and had the door bolted against him. So he came back and shoulder charged the door and completely shattered it. They were tough as well as rough. They wanted a strong landlord in there, so when grandfather, who was quite a big man, went to see Mr Kidd at Dartford he got the job.

In those days, before the First World War, there were no restrictions on opening hours and when the wood-cutters were on the beer, at weekends or after they'd been paid, they'd be on the doorstep at six o'clock in the morning waiting for the pub to open. And if they fancied a beer while they were working, they always had the excuse that they were going to the pub to grind their axe, as the *Fox and Hounds* had a grindstone at the back. It was a treadle one that was there for ages. A woodman would stop work, look at his axe and say 'I'm just going to the pub to have a grind' and that would be his excuse to go on the beer. And they didn't go in the pub for half a pint, they would order half a gallon. The landlord would put two quart pots on the bar for them. If they were hungry they might buy some bread and cheese and a pennorth of pickles from the jar. Grandfather's way of dealing with them was quite simple – if they turned difficult he would stop serving them. And he was tough enough to stand up to them. Wood-cutters and farm workers were his main customers. And, as I said, before the First World War he would get the charcoal burners who came every year to Leize Wood.

Lord Dunsany at Dunstall owned the freehold at the *Fox and Hounds*. Kidd's Brewery from Dartford leased it. Captain Kidd, who owned Kidd's Brewery, was master of the West Kent Hunt and a magistrate at Dartford. After Kidd's lease expired, Courage took over the pub in 1936. When Lord Dunsany died in 1957, the brewer didn't want another long lease and so it was sold. It's a free house now.

There wasn't really a living from the *Fox and Hounds* and grandfather had a struggle to survive. He had a field at the back, where the caravans are today, and he kept a few animals there – I mentioned the pigsties. He also kept some cows. But he would have to do seasonal work like hoeing and haymaking, or go to work in the woods to supplement his income, leaving his wife Ellen to run the pub. It was quite common for a publican to have to take some other work. He was always complaining, 'I have to work all week for the privilege of selling beer on a Sunday.' He later got a job at Norton's Mill in Eynsford. He would have to leave very early for that so my father, as a boy, had to milk the cows at the *Fox and Hounds* before himself walking down Bower Lane to school in Eynsford. But as soon as my father left school at 14 and was earning, grandfather didn't want to do any other work. He wanted to live on father.

In fact when my father married, in 1918, grandfather Hollands really resented it. He and grandmother Hollands didn't get on with my mother. The grandparents were always dragging my father back to the pub to help them after he'd left home and got married. I can remember when I was a child, in the 1920s and '30s, we were always being called in to help. Especially when we lived at Romney Street ourselves, in the end part of the pub, which was then a cottage. Father would do a day's farm work then have to go and help them, washing glasses and so on. I was regarded as free labour too. Being attached to the pub, you were always aware of it, not just for the extra work. My younger sister Chrissy and I had a bedroom at the front and we could hear the noise from the bar. It was something we got used to and generally it didn't bother us but, occasionally, at holiday times, the men would get a bit boisterous and make a lot of noise. They didn't have any musical instruments, but they would stand around and clap and sing. And a ploughman, known as 'Old Ricey', would clog dance. Old Ricey always wore cord trousers and big hobnail boots. The boots had metal toe plates and heel irons and he would dance on the stone floor of the bar and strike sparks. And as the men sang louder and clapped harder, Ricey would stamp more furiously on the flagstones, and the vibrations would go right through the building so that me and Chrissy could feel them in our bedroom. Chrissy would get scared but I would say 'Don't worry, it's only Old Ricey dancing.'[7]

My grandparents were glad we were living next door in the 1930s because suddenly the *Fox and Hounds* got busy with a new clientele. Train fares were cheap and at weekends droves of people used to catch a train out of London to Eynsford, their first bit of real countryside, and they'd walk up over the hills to the pub. Then they'd go back via Shoreham or Otford stations. On a summer Sunday, or a bank holiday, there were hundreds of people up here. The war finished that habit and it never returned. Today I can go down through Magpie Bottom on a Sunday and see three people where I used to see three hundred. But in the days when the *Fox and Hounds* was full of day trippers at weekends, living near the pub was a thorough nuisance for us; we were called in to help all the time.

The farmers cashed in on all those visitors to the area too. At Romney Street Farm, Mr Elcome used to let out a field for camping and he'd have it full of tents at a tanner a head per night. He could make his rent for the farm out of that. Romney Street is a hilly farm, and he didn't let out the best fields; they'd have to camp on a rough, steep one. Like nearly all this area, Romney Street Farm is very high; you can see right up to London. Back in the mid-19th century a sailor, Captain Burton, owned Romney Street Farm and he would fly his flag there amongst some tall fir trees, so that when his ship was anchored on the Thames he could spot his flag from the ship.

My grandparents had a daughter, May, living with them at the pub, but she got fed up with providing free labour too and, when she left, my father got dragged in more and more. He was too near by. Grandfather Hollands stayed at the *Fox and Hounds* till his late seventies and, of course, he'd never paid for a pension, so he used to keep saying to my father 'You'll have to make us an allowance'. But father had his own family to support – myself and my sister – and he was only a farm worker himself, so he didn't earn much. Grandmother Ellen Hollands died at the *Fox and Hounds* in 1943. In 1944 grandfather Horace gave up the tenancy and moved to a cottage a couple of doors away. He died soon after.

After grandfather left, my uncle on the Morgan side, Arthur, took over the pub. Arthur was always known as 'Chummy' Morgan. He then had the pub for 17 years. He used to go out to work and his wife Issel, and daughter Salena, mainly looked after it. Lord Dunsany still owned the pub and they had to leave it as it was – they had oil lamps in there instead of electricity because that's the way Lord Dunsany wanted it. Lord Dunsany had a thing about electricity – he didn't trust it. I was told that when he went to the dentist in Sevenoaks he would wrap newspaper around his head to protect his brain from the electric drill!

During the war, Chummy worked at Vickers armaments factory at Dartford. That was a big employer. As it was a reserved occupation some men preferred working there to joining the army, but that wasn't the case with Arthur, as he was too old for service anyway. After Vickers he worked in the woods, and later he worked on the Highfield Estate for the Cohens. When his wife Issel died, in 1960, Arthur didn't stay on at the pub much longer. He moved in to a cottage on the Highfield estate. The Cohens had quite a bit of land, and some wood, but they were legal people and farming as such wasn't their business. They had their own cows to provide milk and butter to the house, and they sold a bit of farm produce. They would also fatten a cow and send it to market. They also had chickens for eggs, which either went to the house or were sold cheaply to the estate workers. But farming wasn't their living. Sir Herbert Cohen was involved with the West Kent Hunt and they used to meet at Highfield on Boxing Days. He had two sons, Nigel and Stephen. Nigel was mad keen on flying. He had a Gipsy Moth up here. In fact this area has always had quite a strong association with flying.

One of the earliest pioneers of flight, Percy Pilcher, used to carry out his flying experiments up this way right back in the 1890s. That was at Round Hill, near Upper Austin Lodge. If you go down the footpath beside Romney Street Farm you can see across to Round Hill from the stile. Grandfather Morgan could remember Pilcher running and taking off from the Knob, which is across from Round Hill, in his glider, a hang-glider with wings made of bamboo and fabric. The locals christened him 'the wings man'. Grandfather said he got his men to pull him from one hill to another with a tow rope made of fishing line. He could get up to forty feet off the ground and glide about two hundred yards. At a demonstration he gave here in 1897, for scientific people, he got even higher. After he moved away from Eynsford he designed a powered machine with a small petrol engine and a propeller. But before he could test it he was killed giving another gliding demonstration in 1899. Who knows what he would have done if he hadn't been killed? Pilcher originally worked for Hiram Maxim, the machine-gun man based at Crayford. Maxim used the Round Hill area as a firing range. They would put up a red flag if people came along the footpath from Romney Street, to tell the guns to stop.

In the First World War, a field just north of Romney Street was known as the 'flying field'; planes came in and out of there. There was also an airfield at Farningham, near the railway line. Once an officer was brought back to Farningham directly from the Western Front because his mother was dying. When he got off the plane his uniform was still covered in red mud. The

Round Hill area was also used a lot by gliders and small planes later on. We used to come and watch them when I was a small boy in the 1920s. I saw one plane crash near Romney Street Farm and the pilot was killed – he was burned. Going back to the Cohens, Sir Herbert's son Nigel was also killed in a crash. He liked doing stunts, and he crashed his plane down at Hythe after going in to a very fast dive. The wing collapsed under the pressure, apparently. Even today up here there's still a little airstrip behind Romney Street Farm. The other Cohen son, Stephen, died during the war. He contracted a disease in India. That was the line wiped out, so Highfield eventually passed to the Waley-Cohens from Devonshire. They turned Highfield into flats and sold a lot of it off. When the estate broke up, Arthur had to move out and got a council place at Shoreham.

The other pub up here, the *Rising Sun*, was in the Bensted family for about 90 years, from John Bensted in the 1880s to Jack Bensted who retired in 1976. Old Albert Bensted, Jack's uncle, ran a small smithy there. The forge was at the side of the pub where the car park is now, to the east. I can remember Albert shoeing horses there in the 1920s, but he didn't operate the forge all the time. When they were building Shorehill, Oliver Lyle's mansion, in the 1920s, Albert forged the blades on all the picks for them. When Albert died, Jack Bensted took over the pub. They're all buried at Woodlands. There used to be a proper foundry at Eynsford called Gibsons. They made ploughs, harrows and so on. I remember in wintertime you'd see the flare go up when they opened the furnaces. Charlie Green was apprenticed there as an iron moulder, and his job was considered important enough to be a reserved occupation in the First World War. The foundry was opposite the *Five Bells*. You'll often see things around here with Gibson's name on. At Woodlands Church there's a little metal cross that leans against the wall by the porch. It's from a young boy's grave and written on it is 'Gibson's of Eynsford'.

Going back to the family, my father Horace Hollands grew up in this area, as I said. He was born in 1892 and was a child when grandfather Hollands took on Park House Farm in the 1890s. I've mentioned he went to Eynsford School, even after the family had moved to the *Fox and Hounds* in 1904. Father would have left school in 1906 and started doing farm work. In fact that's all he ever did, farm work.

His first job was in 1906 at Dunstall Farm, working for Mr Carter. He worked there until he got married. He was still living at the pub because the farm didn't have a cottage, and when he started he was only a 14-year-old

13 Horace Hollands, Jack's father. Horace worked on farms on the hills all his life. As a young man he drove animals to and from market. This photograph was taken in the 1920s when he was head herdsman at Porter's Farm.

boy anyway. One of the things he had to do was drive animals to and from the markets. From Dunstall he would have to drive them to and from Tonbridge market. He had a hard drive once when Carter had bought some sheep at Tonbridge and wanted father to bring them back the next day. He said to father 'Get up here at 5 o'clock, and I'll take you and the dog down in the trap and you can bring the sheep home'. Father said he set off from Tonbridge with them and made reasonable progress, and when he got to the top of Sevenoaks, and heard the clock strike one, he thought he was doing alright. Then it came on to rain and the sheep's wool got wet, and once the wool gets wet it gets very heavy and the sheep get tired. From there on it took him *hours* to get to Dunstall. The sheep slowed right down you see, with the weight of all that soggy wool.

He used to drive animals quite a lot. Later, when he worked at Woodlands Farm, he would drive them through Knatts Valley to Dartford market. He often had to get up early to drive some bullock to Dartford.

It's surprising the distance they drove animals. One of the ways farmers up here earned some money was by keeping other people's sheep during the winter. A lot of sheep would be brought up here all the way from Romney Marsh, right across the county. That was because Romney Marsh itself used to get waterlogged in the winter and the land couldn't support the year's new breed. By the way, the name Romney Street has got nothing to do with that – I think it's named after people who farmed there.[8] Anyway, they would bring up about a thousand sheep from Romney. They'd drive them over three or four days as far as Wrotham. Then the Romney drovers had to walk back. When they got home they had to cut the laces off their boots to get them off, their feet were so swollen. There are still some reminders of the days of the drovers in this area. Pubs called the *Ship* were often originally called the *Sheep*. At Cobham, to the north-east, there is a pub called the *Ship* which is near Halfpence Lane. A halfpenny is what the drovers paid to pasture their animals in a field at night – a halfpenny per head. At Sutton-at-Hone there is a long lane called 'Ship Lane' which was probably 'Sheep Lane'. A couple of pubs to the east used to be called the *Drovers*. From Wrotham the blokes from up here would go and fetch the sheep the last leg of the journey. My father used to do that. Then they'd share them out, one farmer would have 200, another 300 and so on. After wintering up here they were sent back the following spring, but the farmers were only paid for the ones they returned. If they let any die they weren't paid for those. I can remember the last of the sheep from Romney coming up here in about 1926, when my father was working at Porter's Farm. They had 300 sheep to keep over that winter. The sheep owners from Romney would come up to inspect them. My uncle Wally, as a boy, would take them round the various fields and show them the sheep and he'd be given half a crown for taking them round. I'm told that sheep from Romney are still taken to places like Tatsfield, just along the Downs.

Father worked at Dunstall Farm through the First World War and didn't join the army, partly because he was in a reserved occupation but mainly because of his bad eyesight – like mine. He was only grade two or three, so they reckoned he was doing more good where he was. At the end of the war he went to work for Sam Clark at Woodlands Farm. Father wanted to get married and Sam Clark had a cottage there, one of the flint farm cottages. Father married Edith Morgan on Boxing Day, 1918, at Woodlands Church. People often got married on Boxing Day. Sam Clark rented Woodlands Farm from Julia Vincent, the daughter-in-law of John Painter Vincent, who had owned Woodlands Manor and rebuilt the church. Julia Vincent still owned the whole Woodlands estate. Father did general farm work there. It wasn't very prosperous; they used to grow potatoes and fatten animals. The land was very hilly, as the golf course it was turned into is today.

Sam Clark grew potatoes on the only flat field he had. His men would sometimes dig out the whole crop by hand. My father helped do that. On that sort of job, as you worked, your fork would get caked with mud, so the men carried a little wooden implement called a 'spudger' to scrape the mud off. They also carried this when they were hoeing; it would be stuck in the leg of their trousers. I don't know if that's how Spudgers Pond got its name – it was also called Spuddes Pond at one time. To keep their cord trousers clear of their muddy boots they used to hitch their trousers up at the knee with yokes – bits of string tied around the trousers. It was a tough living and really only subsistence farming. Father said they used to make up their money by catching rabbits.

The farmers here did make a bit of money when things were short during the First World War, and just after, but in the 1920s it went downhill again. After the First World War, London desperately wanted milk, so they all went into dairy farming. They all kept a couple of dozen cows and sent the milk into London. After that war you got a lot of army officers with their gratuities who went into farming. The old estates were being broken up and sold, usually because of death duties, and these officers had some money and saw that farming was quite prosperous – it always is during and just after wars – so they put their money into farming. Major Drummond bought Weike Farm and changed the name to Littlehurst Farm. Captain Hunn came up to Porter's Farm and rented that. Woodlands estate was broken up and sold in 1920. After he'd had a go at farming there, Major Alston started Woodlands Manor Golf Club. As more Woodlands land was sold off, Greves Mellor bought a piece and opened the Woodlands Holiday Camp in 1927.

Knatts Farm and East Hill Farm were sold in 1922 to Homesteads Ltd., and most of the land was split up into little plots of between one to seven acres. These were advertised in the evening papers. The idea of small plots originally was that they were supposed to provide smallholdings for ex-soldiers on which to subsist. There was a government scheme to encourage that idea. But the land was very heavy and not easy to work, as well as being overrun with rabbits. One ex-soldier found the land such hard going he said the smallholdings should have been given to the Germans as a punishment. Many of the plots were re-sold as sites for holiday homes or 'weekend plots'. Quite a few people from London bought them for that. Some of the smallholdings were along East Hill Road and some in the woods. Ashen Grove and Cherry Tree Grove were new roads made for people with plots in those woods. People would put anything on them – wooden huts, even a London bus. There was no water or electricity; services like that didn't come until the 1950s. A man called Pinney lived in a bus on the plot next to this bungalow. When other people bought the plot later they tried to get planning permission but it was refused because the plot had never been rated. Old Pinney had never paid rates so they didn't class it as a residential plot. Over time, the huts and buses and whatever have been replaced by houses and bungalows.

Major Hesketh had a bungalow called 'Crossroads' built up here when East Hill Farm was broken up. He bought several of the Homestead plots and started a poultry farm.

As I said, I was born in 1920 in one of the farm cottages at Woodlands when father was working there. The cottages are high up on the bank in Tinkerpot Lane, now called Woodlands Cottages. After a time we left and he went to work at Porter's Farm for Captain Hunn, who I mentioned earlier. We moved to Goodbury Cottage then. One reason we left was because mother got fed up with pushing a pram up and down the steep steps at Woodlands Farm Cottage – there used to be just earth steps up that high bank beside the road. Father was head herdsman at Porter's Farm. They had about thirty or forty cows there. It was one of the first farms to join the tuberculin-tested milk scheme. Father was well known for being up-to-date on that. The narrow topped pail he has in the photograph was one of the requirements for TT milk. With an ordinary pail, dirt and everything else could get in. To help him run things at Porter's there were some dairymaids who lived in the farmhouse. Also working there was Old Ricey, the ploughman, the one who clog danced in the *Fox and Hounds*. Ricey said he still had the energy for dancing after a day's ploughing because when he ploughed he would rest his hands on the plough handles and let his legs swing like pendulums. We were fond of Ricey in our family because he was a kindly chap. One winter's evening my father had taken the milk from the afternoon milking into Sevenoaks in the old Ford lorry they had and he hadn't come back. It was dark and my mother was getting worried when Old Ricey knocked at the door. He had a hurricane lamp in his hand and some trace chains over his shoulder. He said father had broken down at the bottom of Fackenden Lane so he was going with his horses to tow father home. I thought that was really kind of Ricey, not just to help father, but to think to call in and put mother's mind at rest. Ricey died in 1936 one afternoon, just sitting by the roadside.

Captain Hunn did all right for a while with the dairy farm because he was in with the local doctors. He got them to recommend his tuberculin-tested milk for babies, so that helped his business. But he employed a housekeeper at Porter's and he liked to go riding to hounds quite a lot so the enterprise didn't last too long in that style.

When I first started school I went to Kemsing for a while. I went with Frank Ford, who lived at Clarke's Green. His father was a gardener for Oliver Lyle at Shorehill. I hadn't been at Kemsing long when they started running

14 Romney Street Methodist Chapel, *c.*1930. Jack's forebears helped collect the flints from which it was built in the 19th century. In the 1930s the children's favourite preacher was Mr Skevington, who was 'so loud you could hear him all down Romney Street'.

a bus from here to Eynsford School. That was laid on by Dartford Council. The majority of children up here came under Dartford district, and a lot of those who had come down from London to live here weren't attending school because their parents said it was too far to walk. So when Dartford laid on the bus, my mother put me on that and sent me to Eynsford School. The bus was a charabanc, with a folding hood on the top and curtains round the sides. So most of my schooldays were spent at Eynsford. There were a lot of children up here and in the holidays we played around quite a bit. Father would sometimes take me thatching with him, and I did a bit of bird-minding on Elcome's strawberry fields at Romney Street. Elcome employed a lot of old boys at a tanner an hour and they only did as much work as they felt like.

On Sunday afternoons I used to go to the Romney Street Methodist chapel. It's still there in the garden behind the corner cottage. It's built out of large, unknapped flints – some of my family, old Tiny Groombridge's daughters, helped collect those flints off the local fields when the chapel was built in the 19th century. They were following the style of the medieval Maplescombe Church, built of flints. The Methodist services were originally held in the farmhouse at Romney Street. Then Bavo Booker's family had the chapel built. The old travelling Methodist preacher used to say it was the tiniest chapel he preached at. He'd have to walk over the hills to reach it. The Bookers eventually gave it to the Methodist Church. There's a flint shed next to it which used to be a cottage.

I went to Sunday school more than I did church. Us children would go to the chapel for Sunday school at 2.30 p.m., which preceded the service at 3 o'clock. If somebody we liked was going to be preaching we would stay for the service. The Sunday school teachers were Mrs Bastable and Mrs Green. The Bastables had Littlehurst Farm, previously called Weike Farm, and they were very strong Methodist people. Their children were my contemporaries and they encouraged me to go there. We got quite a good crowd in when the Bastables were running it – if you get someone enthusiastic it drives it along. But once they left it went downhill. It probably closed in the 1960s.

They only had one minister on the Sevenoaks circuit and he came up to Romney Street occasionally, but we usually had lay preachers. Miss Powell, a schoolmistress from Shoreham, came up and preached. We knew her, so we stayed for her. And Mr Wheeler, the baker from Sevenoaks; as well as preaching he used to supply all the cakes for the chapel parties. We got a very good selection. He used to park his baker's van by the chapel and bring the trays out – really nice cakes they were. But our favourite lay preacher was Mr William Skevington, who had the brickworks at Kemsing station. We always stayed for his services because we liked to hear him shout. He was very loud. If the window shutters were open you could hear him all down Romney Street. He used to wave his hands and get really carried away. One Sunday he preached for an hour – we thought that was great entertainment. My mother knew the Skevingtons because she had been in service with them. She had been in service quite a bit before she got married.

I might go to Woodlands Church on some of the special occasions. It could look quite pretty in there. At Easter they would decorate the church with bunches of primroses stuck on moss. You still get masses of primroses today down at Magpie Bottom. And they'd put primroses and daffodils in the church windows. Edna Jupp from Knatts Valley did a lot of the decorating. Her father, Joseph Jupp, kept pigs and chickens. He used to wear a straw hat that was all frayed at the edges and we always said the chickens had been pecking at this hat. At Harvest Festival there was masses of produce because everyone grew stuff up here. The Rev. Milner, another popular vicar at Woodlands, was famous for his marrows.

After Captain Hunn packed up at Porter's Farm, father went to work at Shorehill Farm. When Oliver Lyle, the sugar baron, had the Shorehill complex built he modernised Shorehill Farm for Bill Smith who was the tenant farmer there. Shorehill House itself took six years to build, between 1921 and 1927. Apparently Sir Oliver had first got to know this area as a boy when his family rented Shoreham Place one summer from the Mildmays. He bought the Shorehill site and a large chunk of the North Downs when the old Beechy Lees estate was sold off in about 1919. Time and expense didn't seem to matter to him. With its tower and courtyard, and all the outbuildings, Shorehill is like a French chateau. Men spent months collecting flints for the building from local fields and knapping them by hand. Inside were marble floors and walnut panelling and mosaic bathrooms. It was all very luxurious. When it was finally finished they ran a flag up the chimney and Oliver Lyle took all the workers by special train for a celebration outing to Hastings. But a lot of the men disgraced themselves by getting drunk and falling asleep on the beach. Some were locked in the carriages on the way back.

Quite a few men from up here worked on building Shorehill. One of them was mother's youngest brother, my uncle Wally Morgan. When the Lyles finally moved in, Oliver Lyle said to Wally 'I shall want a chap to look after the generators, are you interested?' Wally said he was, so he had to go up north to learn how to run the big diesel generators in the engine rooms. Shorehill was designed to be self-sufficient, with its own power, own water supply from a 500-foot well, and its own huge kitchen garden. As well as looking after the generators, Wally was a chauffeur. Lyle had two or three chauffeurs. They certainly needed the generators in their first winter of 1927/28 because that was when the 'big snow' came. This area is easily cut off by snow and it was really bad then. The milk from the farms had to be taken down to Shoreham station by sledge. And, knowing things were desperate up here, the baker from Sevenoaks put a sack of bread on the train to Shoreham and that was brought up by sledge. Being so high, 600-700 feet above sea level, the snow is always worse up here and hangs around longer.

But going back to Bill Smith at Shorehill Farm, he had been tenant there since Beechy Lees days, when the Field family had their estate on the hills. The Fields' country house is now St Michael's School. Oliver Lyle built a model dairy for Shorehill Farm, with concrete stands for the cows. The building was thatched with Norfolk reeds, so even the cowshed was luxurious! Today the cowshed is a house called 'Thatched Cottage'. Bill Smith and his sons had

Shorehill Farm for forty-odd years. Anyway, Bill Smith wanted a cowman so father went to work for him. They produced milk to send to London. At least father always had a regular job. Sometimes the men up here were scratching around for work and, to help them out, Bill Smith might employ one for a while catching rabbits. There were always plenty about. Once Harold Clark asked for some work and Bill said 'I've got nothing but you can spend a few weeks catching rabbits'. So Harold would set his wires and catch plenty of rabbits which Bill would pay him for. But sometimes he'd go to his wires early in the morning and find nothing there. Someone had helped themselves to the rabbits. One of the worst offenders was Bill Bunce at Shorehill Cottage, Oliver Lyle's head gardener. Harold would know it was him because he could trace the footprints in the dew. They led back to Shorehill Cottage. Harold confronted Bill Bunce one time but he denied all knowledge. Bill Bunce was well looked after by Oliver Lyle but for some reason he thought he should have *everything*, even someone else's rabbits.

Father was still working at Shorehill Farm when I left Eynsford School in 1934. We were living in Romney Street then. I went to work with father at Shorehill, looking after the dairy cows. By then old Mr Smith had died and his son, another Bill Smith, had taken over. Also working there was the ploughman, Tommy Haffenden, who lived in Otford. Tommy had originally worked at Otford forge, where he was a nailer. The blacksmith would set the horseshoe and the nailer would nail it on. But Tommy was too fond of drink, so they sacked him and he came to work at Shorehill. He would walk up Row Dow to work every day. But he was still fond of a drink and he would often miss work on a Monday and say it was because his legs had 'refused duty'.

Because it belonged to Oliver Lyle, Shorehill Farm, with its model dairy, was really up-to-date compared with all the others. But I got fed up with working seven days a week, as you have to with dairy cows. Father and I had to go in at 6 a.m. every morning to milk a couple of dozen cows, and we had the calves to feed and the yearlings to follow on. So we had forty or fifty animals to look after, and everything was done by hand – there were no milking machines or tractors. I wanted a change and left. Father stayed a while longer and Uncle Wally worked at Shorehill House till he retired.

I had a few jobs after Shorehill. One was at Lullingstone Silk Farm at Lullingstone Castle. That would be in 1937 – I was only there seven or eight months. Lady Zoë Hart Dyke had set that up, but I think Sir Oliver Hart Dyke designed it all because he was an engineer. I expect he had seen how it was done it Italy. I planted the mulberry trees that the worms fed on. The worms would wind themselves with a silk thread into their cocoon. Then you had to bake the cocoon in a kitchen range to kill the worm. Although they provided some of their own cocoons at Lullingstone, a lot of them came from Italy, ready baked, in big sacks like hop pokes. About eight girls worked there in the old laundry. They'd take a cocoon and put it in a sink full of hot water, find the thread, and wind it off. Then there were other girls at the top who were skeining with some machines. They produced little skeins of silk thread. I don't really know the whole process because I wasn't there long enough to see a full cycle of production. I know they later made the queen's wedding dress out of Lullingstone silk. Lady Zoë divorced Sir Oliver and took her silk farm to Esher. I think it's still going today, at Sherborne in Dorset. The Hart Dykes weren't very rich; they'd sold off a lot of land. One of the reasons I left was because I wasn't very good at saying 'Yes my lady' or 'Yes Sir Oliver'. That didn't suit me. Not long after I left Shorehill Farm, father left too. He went to work on different farms.

Just before the war he went to work for Mr Banfield at Austin Lodge Farm. Banfield wasn't really a farmer, he was a developer. He had bought the farm in the late 1930s and he told father he intended to develop it. He wanted to make a road right through to Magpie Bottom. The golf course goes out there today. He hadn't done much with the land – he just kept a few sheep and cut turf for some sports grounds he ran. But because of the war he was made to plough it up and grow wheat. I haven't mentioned wheat growing much because it was never a big thing up here. The big crop was hay, as I've said. The large fields of wheat were down in the valleys. But the farmers on the hills did grow a bit, to feed the corn to their horses, and use the straw for bedding and thatching.

In grandfather Morgan's time they had horse-drawn machines to cut the wheat, but before that it was cut by hand. A gang of reapers went across the corn field cutting it in swathes, and women followed behind tying the corn into sheaves. These were stacked in stooks of ten. That was so that when they were gathered in, one sheaf from each stook was left behind for the parson's tithe. Earlier in the 19th century, his share would be taken to the tithe barn at Shoreham, which stood in what is now the north-west part of the graveyard. Before being collected, the stooks were left to stand in the field for three clear Sundays, to let the corn harden off and dry. Modern combines have to have driers to take out the moisture as they go.

When father was a boy, in the 1890s, they had reaping machines pulled by three horses. The cut corn was pushed off the machine and landed in a lump in rows. Then the bondmakers, mostly women again, would come behind and tie it into sheaves. The women would usually wear wide-brimmed hats because in Victorian times apparently it wasn't fashionable to have a suntan. The sheaves were then made into round stacks. If it was going to be some time before the threshing machine could come to separate the corn, the stacks would be thatched. My father was good at stack thatching. Mother remembered the excitement of the self-binding reaper, which appeared up here around 1900. That threw out bound sheaves of corn. All the children liked to watch that at work. The sails of the reaper were painted either red or blue. In this area they were usually painted blue. The machines up here probably belonged to Jimmy Cole at Porter's Farm, who ran a contracting business, cutting for other farmers, so he had good machinery.

So there was a limited tradition of wheat growing up here, but not on a big scale. And yet when they were told to grow wheat at Upper Austin Lodge Farm for the war effort, they grew wonderful crops. Father had about forty stacks to thatch. He used to take me with him. I used to have to draw out the straw for him and put it in the wooden 'dogs' for him to take up the stack. I've never thatched myself, but I know how it's done. I watched father do it and you can learn fairly easily. By the time he was working at Austin Lodge, he was using a thatching needle instead of the old wooden splints. He'd sew the straw on with binder twine – it saved a lot of work. When they were dismantling a corn stack or cutting up a haystack the rats would come running out. The local ratcatcher would put up a fence of wire netting around the stack to trap them, then he'd hit them with a stick. Sometimes the rats would jump over the fence in desperation. After a year or two of wheat growing at Austin Lodge they had too much straw, and Banfield said to father 'What can we do with all this straw?', so father told him he could fat some animals. So they built up a bullock yard. They enclosed an area with wire netting on poles, filled it with straw and put 30 yearlings in there. Then, as the bullocks made dung, they'd keep putting more straw on and eventually all of that would be spread on the land. By the end of the war father had all these bullocks to look after, and he had a seven-day-week job again. He had to walk down there from Romney Street on Sundays to feed the bullocks, but it wasn't as bad as milking.

During the war the agricultural committees made farmers plough up every bit of land they could. Some of the large fields had been ploughed in the First

World War. They did that with steam ploughs, an engine either side pulling the plough across on a cord. I saw them still doing that in the 1920s and '30s on the bigger fields. But some of the fields up here I doubt had *ever* been ploughed. They were just pasture. Still, if the agricultural committee said a field had to be ploughed, then it had to be ploughed. William Alexander from Eynsford was the chief assessor up here. He'd tell the farmers to plough that field and plant wheat, or plough that one and plant flax. Poor Mr Bath only had two horses, and the committee told him to plough a field and he said 'I can't do it, I can't afford it'. So Alexander said 'It's got to be ploughed. I'll send in a plough, and it will be seeded, and we'll take the crop off and deduct what it's all cost, and you'll get what's left'. As I mentioned, they were still ploughing the land with horses here right up to the war. It wasn't until these big American tractors started to come over on lease-lend in 1942 that they got tractors. The farmers started getting prosperous because the government wanted them to plough up everything and, as in the First World War, they got paid quite well for their produce. That continued for some years after the war too.

Although my eyesight was as bad as my father's, I was called up to the army in 1940 when they thought there was going to be an invasion. They called us all up then, whatever condition. We were given a gun and were soldiers in three weeks. I had to go to North Wales in the Pioneer Corps. Then I went to Warminster. There was a tank trap dug right across the countryside near Frome and we had to guard that. After a year they discharged me because of my eyesight. In 1941 I went to work for Ashby's coal merchants at Shoreham and I carried on there until I retired.

After his time at Upper Austin Lodge, father came back and worked at Romney Street Farm. They had a couple of horses there and he looked after them, as well as doing general farm work. The farm itself passed through two or three hands. A Scotsman called Barclay came there and kept Ayrshire cows. But father didn't work with the cows much because they had milking machines. Barclay rented Romney Street Farm first, then he had Littlehurst, then Porter's. He used to show his pedigree Ayrshires at the Olympia Dairy Show. Eventually he moved away to Hastings. One old skill father did keep up was stack thatching, because they hadn't yet got round to using plastic bags. They also had a Dutch barn, which they filled. They had so much corn they had to store it until threshing. It was while working at Romney Street Farm that father had a heart attack when he was 64. He didn't do any more serious work after that.

We had been living in a cottage that belonged to Romney Street Farm, but we could see the way the wind was blowing on farms, so we bought this bungalow, 'Clovelly', at East Hill in 1952. Farms were beginning to break up, and they didn't want men, and tied cottages were becoming a thing of the past. We bought this place just before father had the heart attack. I felt quite secure at the time with my job at Ashby's coal merchants.

I mentioned that when they sold off the plots on East Hill back in the 1920s there were no services. We only got piped water to this place in the 1950s. They'd had it in some areas that came under Dartford control since 1936, but we came under Sevenoaks and they didn't provide it until the '50s. The Sevenoaks/Dartford border is just down East Hill Road. The dustmen used to call one day to one half and another day to the other half.

Water has always been a problem up here, there's no natural supply. There are some ponds, but no streams. There are a few deep wells. At East Hill Farm the old well goes down 350 feet; that's how far they had to go to get water. In the 1920s at Shorehill, which is higher, they had to go down a lot further. I reckon their well shaft goes down over 500 feet, but there was some dispute about that. The drillers said to Oliver Lyle they would like to go down to greensand, but the equipment wasn't good enough and it broke. Some people got the sack over it, and they had to get one of their well shooters in to recover the tackle. He said they'd have to settle for what they'd reached – he reckoned there was a plentiful supply there. I'm not sure how deep it is, and I don't think Oliver Lyle knew the exact truth either, even though the sale catalogue for Shorehill says 400 feet.

Once the water companies started laying on piped water there were a few private pipes up here. East Hill Farm had one, and people from the holiday home plots used to go there with a can and pay to fill it up – a penny for a two-gallon can. Lord Dunsany had a private pipe too, laid on from Clarke's Green. He had that installed in the 1920s and it went to Romney Street, but nobody else could have it because it was his pipe. The *Fox and Hounds* pub got it because that belonged to Lord Dunsany. Anyone else had to pay him for it. In our various cottages we used to have underground tanks to store the rainwater off the roof. Then you had to boil it for drinking.

When I first started work at Shorehill Farm, I used to take a couple of bottles to work and bring them home full of clean water. When father worked at Porter's Farm, which had piped water, he'd fill a bucket with clean water and bring that home. Clean water was precious, you see. The other water from the tanks was all right for washing and suchlike but fresh, clean water – that was precious. When mother was young, of course, there wasn't any tap water anywhere, and they always had to boil their water. If there was a really dry summer, grandfather Morgan would go down to the Darent at Shoreham with a horse and cart and fill up barrels from the stream to bring up here.

As I said, we got piped water in East Hill Road in the 1950s, and when the family bought this bungalow in 1952 we had electricity connected. Main drainage didn't arrive until 1996, but this place still has a cesspit. They want quite a bit of money for connecting you to main drainage.

So we got electricity here, but I mentioned they didn't have electricity at the *Fox and Hounds* in the 1950s. That was because of Lord Dunsany not liking electricity and wanting the pub to stay the way it had always been. So my uncle, Chummy Morgan, wasn't allowed to change anything there when he was landlord. But I don't think that bothered Chummy. He and his wife Issel and daughter Salena ran the place in their own style. They used candles and paraffin lamps for lighting but, in the winter, if there were only a few customers, Chummy would light just the one lamp at their table. So it could be pretty gloomy. People would try to play darts by the light of a candle. Customers may have thought Chummy a bit eccentric. If he ran out of glasses he would serve you your beer in a jam jar, or he might give you a whisky in a Shippam's paste jar. And he had his own way of measuring whisky. He would put his finger in the glass and measure up to the first joint for a single and up to the knuckle for a double. That was probably quite a generous measure. What with the gloom and Chummy's ways, the locals christened the pub 'Jamaica Inn' while he was there. Considering the smuggling associations with the area, that wasn't a bad name.

Like grandfather Hollands, Chummy couldn't rely on the pub for a living and he would have to do other work. So during the day it would be Issel and Salena in charge. Chummy worked at Vickers armaments factory in the war, as I said, and he was also a wood-cutter and grave-digger. He started grave-digging during the war because there was no one else to do it. When grandfather Hollands died, Chummy said he would dig the grave at Woodlands and after that he just carried on. In the 1950s the local policeman was Sergeant Atkinson from Kemsing. Because he was so big he was known as 'Fatty Atkinson'. One day he stopped Chummy coming home from the churchyard because Chummy was covered in mud and carrying a sack with his tools in and Sergeant Atkinson probably thought he looked suspicious.

15   Chummy Morgan at the *Fox and Hounds*, 1950, with wife Issel, left, and daughter Salena, who is drinking from the water jug. Jack's uncle Arthur, known as 'Chummy', ran the pub in his individual way from 1944-61.

He said to Chummy 'What are you up to?'. Chummy eyed him up and down and said 'I'm doing a job I shouldn't like to do for you.' Once, on a really warm summer's day, Chummy got a bit hot grave-digging. So he stopped and went to the *Rising Sun* for a drink. That was nearer than the *Fox and Hounds*. But when he got back there was an Alsatian dog in the grave. He didn't know how to get it out; it was pretty fierce and ready to bite him. The grave had to be dug that afternoon so he had a real problem. Luckily the owner turned up and got it out for him.

Chummy had a little dog of his own and when he worked in the woods he would go by bicycle with the dog in a basket in the front. He always sang while he worked. Once he had to cut down a big tree next to a power line and he misjudged it and it fell against the line. But Chummy wasn't bothered and he carried on stripping it. Somebody said it looked dangerous but Chummy said he'd be all right because he'd come prepared. He had a normal boot on one foot and a Wellington boot on the other. He reckoned if he accidentally touched the power line the one rubber boot would insulate him. Later on he got a BSA motorbike which he rode to and from various jobs. With the noise of the engine he would have to sing more loudly. As he went by people would say 'Why's that old boy hollering?' but that was Chummy singing.

After Issel died in 1960, Chummy didn't stay on at the pub much longer. He went to work on the Highfield estate and he and Salena got a tied cottage there. But when Sir Herbert Cohen died in 1968 they were told to leave. Sir Herbert's cousin, Bernard Waley-Cohen, wanted to modernise the cottages and let them. Even Cyril McQueen, the farm manager who had been on the estate, man and boy, for 50 years, was told to go. It was typical of Chummy that he just laughed and said 'They can't put me out'. But they did and he and Salena finished up in a council house in Shoreham – where they kept a barrel of cider in the shed. Courages had taken over the lease of the pub from Kidd's of Dartford. After Chummy's departure they did it up. When they re-opened it they said in the paper that before it had been a 'desolate place with no civilisation'. That may have been their opinion, but local people liked it. Courages themselves later gave up the lease and it reverted to the Dunsany estate. They then sold it to Unwins who ran it with managers – but no one quite like Chummy. It's still a popular pub today with hikers going over the hills. The cottage at the end where we lived in the 1930s has been incorporated into the pub, so it's quite big. You can see it now has some fake rustic timbering on the front which it never had when it was a real wood-cutters' pub.

By the 1950s, when we had bought our place, some of the other plots from the 1920s which might have originally had just a shack on them had been built on. I suppose, like Chummy, some of the people living up here, away from it all, so to speak, were not your average sort of person. A bit more individual, you might say. In one bungalow, for instance, there was a lady who was mad keen on animals. In fact she moved out of her bungalow into a caravan and let her animals live in the bungalow! She had quite a menagerie there – dogs, cats, a monkey, a fox – all well fed on fresh butcher's meat. She got another caravan to house 20 geese and there were a donkey, two goats and two ponies grazing in the garden. You can imagine it was a bit of a problem for her son when she died. When he came up to sort it out he didn't know what to do. All the furniture had to be burnt. He found homes for most of the animals but I think someone had to poke a gun through the window and shoot the fox – it would never have survived in the wild. The bungalow was eventually demolished. She'd had 15 cats there and when she died they all set off like a great tribe across the hills and just adopted people the way they do. One of them came to our place and I had to feed it. But the funny thing was, when it got old and knew it was dying, it went back to the site of the bungalow to lay down and die there.

Not all the farmers up here were your average farmer either. A chap called Barry Wells took over Littlehurst Farm in the 1960s and ran it on his own, though he really had more land than he could manage. It didn't help that actual farming didn't seem to be his main interest. He spent most of his time watching insects and studying anything dead or diseased. He'd look under a piece of bark and try to identify all the insects. He'd spend half the day doing that instead of getting on with the farm work. If he found a dead animal or a diseased plant, he wanted to know what the cause of it was. So he was always sending off specimens to places like the Natural History Museum. At the post office they got used to him sending odd-shaped parcels with lumps of bark or dead birds inside. But the postmistress drew the line when he came in with a large smelly parcel containing a dead fox. She wouldn't accept it. Barry said he just wanted to know why it had died.

I mentioned dene holes and Barry had one in front of his farm. It was quite a big one and was later filled in – it took several lorry-loads to fill it. Barry said he had been down it and he reckoned it was a flint mine where they got black flint for the old flintlock guns. It could be true. The trouble was Barry didn't devote enough attention to his farm. He never got round to cutting his corn on time. He'd finish up harvesting it in December. Of course by that time there wasn't much left; it had either fallen or the birds had taken it. He'd look like Father Christmas sitting on his combine in his anorak. People would say 'There goes Barry, cutting his Christmas corn'.

Father died here. He was 80 when he died in 1972. Mother lived on another 17 years. I was living at home while I worked at Jimmy Ashby's. He had half a dozen men working at the coal yard by the station when the business was at its peak, before Dr Beeching closed the yard down. After that they had to get coal from Bat and Ball station, or by road. A lot of it was brought directly from the pits – 12-ton lorries would arrive from Welsh coal mines at nine o'clock in the morning. Now my coal comes from China! I left in 1979 when I was nearly 60. Mother had got more and more dependent and she didn't like me going to work. Jimmy Ashby sold out around 1984. Under the next people it folded about three years later. The coal business has shrunk and shrunk. At Sevenoaks station Charringtons have a little bit in the corner, where it used to be full of coal.

I don't know how things are going to go on up here in the future. There is still some serious farming. Mr Hitchcock, at Littlehurst, does dairy farming and has about a hundred cows and 'followers', the young stock. His land now includes the old Romney Street Farm. The only crops he grows are maize and grasses for cattle feed. You could say he still lives entirely off the land, but the other big farms have been broken up and, where people still do some farming, they don't totally depend on it, and have other interests to make a

16   Jack's bungalow, winter 2005/06. It is currently awaiting re-development.

living – contracting, caravan sites and so on. With farming going the way it is, I suppose people can't afford to depend on it.

Mr Gilman, at East Hill Farm, makes hay and fattens bullocks – he wins lots of prizes with them. He still has quite a bit of farmland, but he also has mobile home sites. At Porter's Farm, Mr Hodges also fattens bullocks and makes hay to feed them, but his main business is agricultural contracting – ploughing, combining, baling, hedge-cutting – he does all the labour for other farmers. It saves the small farms employing people and buying machinery. A few of the others are 'dog and stick' farmers – grazing animals and walking round with a dog and stick. Recently, horse pasturing has become popular. I suppose it's a way to make some money from the land. At Bavo Booker's last place, Broomy Croft, which is now called Bali Hai, they go in for horse livery where he used to run a hay and wood business. Of course Woodlands Farm became a golf course and for some years there was a holiday camp on a bit of the Woodlands estate. That's now built over. Austin Lodge has become a golf course, so perhaps these leisure activities, like golf and horse riding, will take over more and more from farming.

There are still just a few sheep, but nothing like the flocks that used to be kept. The number of sheep decreased as the whole area, including the villages below, became more populated. New people moving in weren't country people, and if they kept dogs they didn't realise their dogs would kill the sheep. A lot of sheep were lost because of dogs – and the farmers couldn't stand the losses – that didn't happen before the 1920s and '30s.

The woods are nearly all derelict now; they're not properly managed. As I've told you, the woods used to be a thriving industry, but there's not much activity today. You can still see fallen trees lying from the 1987 gale. At Birchin Cross there's a bit of chestnut, which was cut some years ago and is growing up again like it should be, and at Highfield they've planted some conifers – there's a market for those I suppose. But generally the woods are not so well looked after. They might cut some of it for pulp, or take a bit of firewood, but it's not managed like it was in grandfather Morgan and Bavo Booker's day. There's no market for the wood products any more – the firelighting faggots, the hurdles, the hop poles and so on.

This is marginal land up here and I think it could become semi-derelict, especially if farming goes on being such a struggle. It's all Green Belt land and the council are strict on planning permission, so at the moment no one can build much. They mostly replace earlier buildings on a one-for-one basis. Those holiday homes from the 1920s and '30s are replaced with modern houses. Some of the transformations have been quite impressive. In Hills Lane there's a smart house called 'The Hut' which originally *was* just a hut with a tin roof. But now it's quite a luxurious place worth over a million pounds. Not exactly what you'd call a hut any more. I can remember the Tassells who lived there when it was a hut. Not all the replacement buildings are like that but they are always bigger, with space for two or three cars, so you get much more traffic.

The old way of life built round working on the land, farming and wood-cutting, has largely gone. It used to be all farm workers up here, but they don't need men on the land any more. And as I've said, the wood business has virtually died out. The government keep saying we need thousands of new homes, but they could only build some here if they completely changed the Green Belt policy. At the moment this area is protected.

After me, there won't be a Morgan or Hollands connection up here. The other old families, like the Bookers and the Clarks, have either moved away or are in the churchyard. As you will have gathered, all my roots are up here, so I've never considered living anywhere else.

Jack died in June 2005. He is buried with his father, Horace, and his mother, Edith, in Woodlands churchyard.

Background to the Area

I have used the term 'East Hill', as Jack did, to describe a general area which is something of a no man's land on the fringe of several parishes. Today it is mainly divided between Shoreham, West Kingsdown, Eynsford and Farningham. The roving palaeontologist, Benjamin Harrison, who searched these hills, once mentioned finding a Neolithic tool in 'no parish' – a field where three parishes met but whose ownership was disputed (1895).[1] It is the area of the North Downs in west Kent above the vale of Kemsing and east of the Darent Valley. Although there is only one farm here actually called 'East Hill', many people use that term as shorthand for this stretch of downland – i.e. the east hill of the Darent Valley.

It seems to have always been an isolated area and yet it is only some twenty miles from London. From the field by East Hill crossroads you can see direct to Canary Wharf. Visitors are always struck by the sense of remoteness so close to the capital. Certainly many of them find it easy to get lost among its network of narrow lanes with high hedges.

There were originally two parishes on the hills, Maplescombe and Woodlands, but both were later absorbed by others. Although Maplescombe's two entries in Domesday Book seem impressive, its tiny church was later abandoned and the parish was subsumed into neighbouring Kingsdown around 1620. Both Maplescombe and Woodlands churches are included in an 11th-century list of churches in the Rochester diocese,[2] but Woodlands Church, too, was left to decay and the parish united with Wrotham in about 1520. A new Woodlands Church was built by an incoming benefactor, John Painter Vincent, in 1850, but Maplescombe Church remains a romantic ruin, its lower flint walls still visible in a field in Knatts Valley. The original Woodlands Church was probably a modest affair, like Maplescombe, serving as it did a small population of poor people. It is thought that the dereliction of the two churches was probably due to the loss of interest in donating to their upkeep after the Reformation.

What was interesting about Jack's story was its direct link to the past and its sense of continuity. The way of life he describes has many echoes of a much earlier period. The workers in the coppice wood we can trace back to Domesday Book. Such woods, *silva minuta*, are referred to in Domesday Book for Kent. There are records of the manor of Maplescombe being re-stocked with sheep in 1186.[3] In Jack's father's time, the pasturing of sheep on the downs was still an important source of income. Although the medieval practice of pasturing pigs in the woodland had disappeared, the keeping of a pig or two in the garden, as Jack's grandfather Horace did at the *Fox and Hounds*, persisted.

Woodlands, as the 'yoke of Wodelond', was an outlying part of the Archbishop of Canterbury's huge manor of Otford. In looking at the services tenants from this area were expected to perform in the 13th century, we can see some affinities with Jack's story. Jack's other grandfather, the waggoner Henry Morgan, regularly transported bundles of fire-lighting faggots from the woods on the hills and, in an Otford Manor Custumal of 1284, it is stated that one obligation of the tenants was to carry loads of firewood to the court at Otford.[4] Another service was to repair the burghyard fence and make hurdles for the lord's enclosure. Jack's wood-cutters were still making hurdles in the 20th century. Help with the haymaking and the corn harvest were other services listed. In Jack's great-great-grandfather's time, the hay and corn would have been gathered in much the same way, cut with scythes and the hay raked and stacked, the corn bound into sheaves and stooked.

The diet of the 13th-century cottars (smallholders) also makes an interesting comparison. When obliged to work on the lord's land they would receive food three times a day. At Prime (early morning) and Vespers (evening) this would be a loaf, a whole cheese and drink, and at the ninth hour a wheat loaf, pottage, cheese and drink. One is reminded of Jack's wood-cutters and their bread and cheese at the *Fox and Hounds* and, more especially, of the simple boiled meals produced by Jack's female ancestors over an open fire in the cottages at Romney Street – offerings which sound very much like medieval 'pottage'.

There was even a leper hospital at Otford in 1228, a grim precursor of the Isolation Hospital in which Jack's uncle Wally was confined.[5]

The Teflynge Yoke, for which some of the above services were listed, probably included the Romney Street area. The Romney Street name derives from early holders of this land. In 1414 Henry and John Romney held 74 acres here and the Romney name crops up regularly in records. In 1533 John Romneys, senior and junior, held land near East Hill Farm.

There have been many owners of the Maplescombe and Woodlands manors, but to give an exhaustive list would be exhausting. At various times they have been in royal ownership and some distinguished families have held them.

In the late 16th century Woodlands was owned by William Rowe, Lord Mayor of the City of London. Maplescombe was owned by the Lovelace and Coke families. But these owners didn't live there; the farms were leased. The Lovelaces were from east Kent and the Cokes lived in East Anglia. Richard Lovelace, the 'Stone walls do not a prison make' poet, was a distant Lovelace cousin, and Henry Coke, an owner of Kingsdown and Maplescombe, was the fifth son of Lord Chief Justice Edward Coke. Some references give an indication of the use of the land. When another Coke, Robert, owned Maplescombe in the 1670s the 'sale of timber in Kent' was noted. He also owned East Hill Farm and it is Robert Coke's initials that can still be seen on the chimney of the farmhouse, with the year '1672'.

In the late 18th century Woodlands and Week Farms were leased to James Luck and his agreement required him to 'repair the hop kiln' at Woodlands,[6] a clear indication of hop-growing, which continued in the area until Jack's day.

The Cokes owned Maplescombe for a long period. In 1776 the estate passed to Thomas William Coke, known as 'Coke of Norfolk', famous for his improvements in crops and stock-breeding. None of these improvements was brought to Maplescombe and East Hill, however, as he sold his estates in Kent. Interestingly, a later agricultural improver, William Boddy, experimented at Dunstall Farm, where Jack's father worked, on the Shoreham side of the hills. In the early 1900s his careful study of white clover eventually led to its seed being sold commercially all over the world.[7]

Intellectual curiosity was not always an asset when farming here, as Jack's description of Barry Wells at Littlehurst Farm in the 1960s shows. Barry lost his farm due to the twin distractions of studying diseased plants and dead animals. At Littlehurst Farm there was a large dene hole which Barry suggested was a flint mine. This may have been so. At nearby Kingsdown in the late 18th century lived James Woodyer, who brought an improved method of making gun flints to England from France. His technique produced better flints and millions were supplied to the army during the Napoleonic wars. Why would some of these flints not have been mined locally?

There is a long tradition of estates in Kent being bought by wealthy Londoners. We have seen that Woodlands was owned in the 16th century by the Lord Mayor of the city, and Maplescombe and East Hill were bought in the 18th century by a city merchant named Duncan Campbell. In the 1830s Maplescombe Farm was owned by John Clarke-Powell, another city merchant investing in country estates. The usual intention seems to have been to make money from rents and the sale of assets like timber. There was also a sporting attraction, as these were areas long associated with hunting and shooting. As early as 1290 one Roger de Mereworth was granted free warren (the right to hunt and preserve game) on his lands at Maplescombe.[8]

Around 1835 the long neglected manor of Woodlands was bought by Londoners with a different motivation. The purchaser was John Painter Vincent, senior surgeon at St Bart's Hospital in London and twice President of the Royal College of Surgeons. But it seems to have been his wife, Eliza Mary, who felt a missionary urge to restore the manor and church and recreate a Christian community in the wilderness. The Vincents first built a new Woodlands Manor House, but Eliza was determined to erect 'a house of God in this place where his name was not known'. Her original discovery of Woodlands and subsequent efforts to get the church rebuilt and 'bring poor benighted souls to Christ' are described in a memoir written in the 1850s (see Appendix). The new Woodlands Church was finally consecrated in July 1850 by the Archbishop of Canterbury. It was built on almost the same site as the abandoned medieval one, using local flints like ancient Maplescombe. The architect was Thomas Talbot Bury, a pupil of Pugin. Inside this pretty church is a memorial to John Painter Vincent and Eliza Mary, which records that the church was 'erected and endowed through their exertions'. Across the top of the memorial is written 'Blessed is he that considereth the poor', so the Vincents clearly felt a Christian duty to help this isolated community rather than merely exploit it. Next to the church a small school was added, the one later attended by Jack's grandfather, Henry Morgan. Finally the handsome flint vicarage was finished in 1859. From here the Reverend John Handcock fulfilled Mrs Vincent's dream of bringing 'poor benighted souls to Christ' during his benign 47-year occupancy. Jack's mother had fond memories of the Rev. Handcock.

The practice of wealthy men adopting a small country community in the role of benevolent 'squire' became a regular phenomenon later in the 19th century. In the valleys below there was almost a competition to see which local squire could be the greatest benefactor of the Victorian and Edwardian villages, providing village halls, recreation grounds, even soup kitchens. Wealthy families continued to take over estates on the hills. The Sugdens bought the Kingsdown estate in the 1860s. They lived locally and took an active interest in village life. When they sold off East Hill and Knatts Farms in 1902 the land was described as 'an agricultural and sporting estate'. Jack's grandfather, Henry Morgan, remembered the Sugdens' shooting parties coming to East Hill.

From early in the First World War, Henry worked for Lord Dunsany, whose family owned the Dunstall estate. Henry managed the large stretches of woodland and kept the rideways open for hunters, but Lord Dunsany, a slightly eccentric author, seems to have been more preoccupied with writing in the woods, in his secluded hut, than hunting in them.

The Highfield estate, bought by MP and philanthropist Sir Benjamin Louis Cohen in 1893, conformed to the pattern of a rich man's country estate, hunted by the West Kent Foxhounds. Although Shoreham, his parish, saw little of him, he gave money to the vicar there to distribute to deserving cases. Jack's family were more aware of the next Cohen at Highfield, Sir Herbert Cohen. Some of Jack's family worked on the Highfield estate, including uncle Harry, whose tragic story is told, and later the singular Chummy Morgan, Harry's younger brother. It was a sign of the times when, after Sir Herbert died in 1968, Chummy and others were told to leave their cottages on the estate at short notice. The days of benefaction were ending; the cottages were modernised and re-let, the big house turned into flats.

There was a burst of selling and breaking up of big estates after the First World War. This was often due to problems caused by death duties, which had been increased by Lloyd George. Sometimes owners had to pay double death duties when an heir had been killed in the war. The Sugdens sold off the rest of the Kingsdown estate in 1919. The Beechy Lees estate, at the southern edge of the area, above Otford, was also sold in 1919. The Woodlands estate, which had passed to absentee owner Julia Vincent, widow of John Painter Vincent's son, was sold in 1920, the year Jack was born. At that time Woodlands Manor House and farm were let to farmer Sam Clark, for whom Jack's father was working, and Jack was born in the farm cottage near Woodlands Church. Although these estates had been owned by wealthy people, the farmers renting the land usually struggled to make a living and the farm workers were distinctly poor. Jack said that it was just subsistence farming on Woodlands Farm in the 1920s. More money was made from the woods than the farms, with the continuing demand for coppice wood products like hurdles and hop poles and fire-lighting faggots.

It was in the 1920s that East Hill and Knatts Farms were resold and much of the land divided into small plots. These were originally intended as smallholdings but they were readvertised in London newspapers as 'weekend plots' and people started to put huts, caravans and, in one case, even a London bus on them. So the estates were breaking up, the character of the area changing and the old way of life of the farmers and wood-cutters, working land owned by the 'local squire', was in retreat.

One man who could afford to keep an estate together, even improve it, was Oliver Lyle, later Sir Oliver, of the Tate and Lyle sugar company. In the 1920s he bought the Shorehill estate above Kemsing, and spent six years building an impressive mansion-cum-chateau which the locals christened 'Treacle Towers'. He also owned a large area of downland and a farm. In fact he wasn't the first sugar merchant to own land here because Duncan Campbell, who bought the Kingsdown estate in 1784, was a dealer in sugar and, quite probably, slaves. Oliver Lyle turned his farm into a model farm and that's where Jack first went to work with his father in the 1930s, looking after the cows. Farm workers like Horace, Jack's father, had always been fairly mobile within a small compass, moving from one farm to another, one tied cottage to another. But Jack was not so keen on farm work, especially dairy farming, where you are on call seven days a week. So eventually he got out of farming and became a coalman, working for Ashby's at Shoreham station.

Jack said he could 'see the way the wind was blowing' on farms. The smaller ones were struggling, only bigger units were viable and the tied cottages were being sold off and modernised. Eventually some of the farm land was turned over to leisure activities like golf, some to horse pasture. There are two golf courses here now, including Woodlands Manor Golf Course, which covers the farmland on which Jack's father was working when Jack was born. As Jack says, the woodland is not now managed in the traditional way as there is no serious demand for the old coppice-wood products. Some woods are still used for shooting, some are now nature reserves and one is used for off-road driving.

So, although this still looks like a largely unspoiled area of farmland and woodland, there has been a gradual shift away from life based around the farms and woods, and a creeping suburbanisation. The makeshift buildings, put on those weekend plots in the 1920s, are replaced by new, larger houses. One of the more impressive million-pound houses retains, in ironic fashion, its original name of 'The Hut'. The new houses generate more traffic, much of it unsuitable for the narrow lanes. One of Jack's constant laments was that he was unable to wander around the area in his accustomed way, looking at the primroses, picking the blackberries, because of the greatly increased traffic.

Jack died in June 2005, and the little bungalow that he and his parents bought in East Hill Road will follow the pattern and be demolished and replaced by a larger house.

With Jack's death we saw the end of the Morgan/Hollands line on the hills, the one family there retaining a link with the distant past. As Jack said when I was recording his story, all the old families, the Bookers, the Clarks, had either moved away or were in the churchyard. Now Jack is there too, buried at Woodlands with his parents, Horace and Edith.

For me it will seem odd not to have Jack to consult whenever some question about life on the hills arises. Apart from his own family story, Jack was a knowledgeable and well-read person on country matters, and was always fascinating to listen to, as much for the authentic Kentish accent and expressive turn of phrase as for the information.

So the purpose of this book is simply to pass on Jack's story in the hope that it will give a picture of life as it was lived by himself and his ancestors on the North Downs, on 'East Hill'.

Appendix

As mentioned, the 11th-century churches of Woodlands and Maplescombe were abandoned in the 16th century. In the early 19th century the Manor of Woodlands itself seemed an abandoned place. But it was acquired around 1835 by the senior surgeon of St Bart's Hospital, London, John Painter Vincent, and a major effort was made to revive the hamlet. A manor house was built and a new church consecrated in 1850. A school and a vicarage were then added. The following account of the resurrection of Woodlands was written in the early 1850s by Eliza Mary, John Painter Vincent's wife. The memorial to them in Woodlands Church says 'the church was erected and endowed through their exertions.'

Woodlands Manor
or Prayer Answered

In a lovely romantic vale, surrounded with hills luxuriantly adorned with wooded scenery, where a stranger is seldom or never seen passing over the beautifully green pathway leading to a neighbouring village, stands a modest manor house; the genuine simplicity of which is most attractive to the eye of such as value rest, retirement, and comfort, unostentatiously provided; whilst its gardens, tastefully laid out, send forth from the flowers therein a most delicious odour truly refreshing, which, accompanied with the exquisitely sweet and pure air wafted by the gentle breeze from hill to hill, and descending to the picturesque valley beneath, invigorates the exhausted frame of such as need rest and enjoy the privilege of visiting this truly favoured abode of peaceful tranquillity.

As the circumstances and history connected with Woodlands Manor are deeply interesting, it is considered desirable that some of the particulars should be made known to those who take real interest in hearing of the providential dealings of God with His people, who trust in Him as a prayer-hearing and prayer-answering God.

The present owner of the Manor was led, from motives unnecessary here to mention, to wish for a retired country residence, which might be occasionally visited, when desirable. Pure air, and all the attractions of rustic scenery were sought for, with as near as possible a proximity to London. Such a place could not easily be found. The metropolis sending forth continually myriads of its inhabitants gasping for fresh air, rendered it next to an impossibility to find a secluded place in the suburbs. What was to be done? The matter was laid before the Lord in humble and believing prayer, the petitioner knowing that He hath said (to His own people), 'If ye shall ask anything in my name I will do it'.

Waiting some time for an answer the offerer of prayer received, one day, an announcement, through a public journal, that an estate was to be sold in Kent. Steps were immediately taken to ascertain its locality, and all particulars respecting it. A visit was paid to the place described, with an anxious desire of ascertaining whether *this* might be the spot prayed for. Arriving at a village some distance from Woodlands, our traveller left her equipage in the care of her servants, and proceeded on foot to find the Manor for which she was in search, as no carriage could possibly go through the narrow and almost impassable winding lanes leading to the vale. The obstructions she met with, even as a pedestrian, told too truly how deserted a place she was in.

After making her way through a stony lane (which she afterwards learned was considered haunted, so that no one dared to go down it) our heroine paused for a while, asking for direction from above. The appearance of the whole place was a desolate, dreary wilderness! Not a soul to be seen! It seemed as though neither man nor any other living creature had ever been there. She felt as if she were hundreds of miles from London, in the most isolated parts of the country. At length her attention was arrested by the sound of what she thought was threshing. Upon examination, she found that there was a very old barn near to the end of the lane through which she had come down; advancing towards it, she perceived an aged man employed in threshing corn. The man looked up with the most surprising stare, at seeing any human being there – especially a lady alone, and unprotected, having come down the haunted lane!

'It is hard work in which you are engaged!' said the lady.

'E'es', replied the man.

'I hope', she continued, 'that you know something of the God who gives us all this corn, and showers down His blessings upon us?'

'I never he-erd of Him', said the man.

'Never heard of God?' exclaimed his enquirer, 'why, in Him we live, and move, and have our being!'

'Na!' again said the man, 'I never he-erd of Him, where does he live?' This led to a conversation which may easily be imagined by those who are interested in the salvation of souls.

Overcome with grief and astonishment at what she had heard, the lady left this poor specimen of heathen darkness, weeping as she retraced her steps towards the place where she had left her carriage, and saying to herself 'Can it be possible? Never heard of God! and this' – will the reader believe it? – 'within twenty miles of London!' Again and again she exclaimed, 'Can it be possible that an immortal soul is perishing for lack of knowledge, so close to the mainspring of missionary enterprise, whence hundreds of missionaries are sent forth to preach the gospel to the heathen?'

With some difficulty, she reached a cottage which she espied in the distance, where was an old man, with whom she entered into conversation. The old man told her that Woodlands had been in that desolate state ever since he knew it, and long before his time. There was no village belonging to it, no church, no chapel near; and that it would never be a fit place for anyone to take, with the intention of building a residence there. The lady asked him about his spiritual state, whether he ever went to a place of worship, even though at a distance from him. He replied that he would gladly go regularly to the house of God, but was often prevented because he was lame and not able to walk so far as the nearest church, and there was no one, whether minister or otherwise, who ever visited in that lone locality, to speak of the things of God.

Returning to London with sorrowful meditations upon the spiritual destitution of the place she had visited, and of which the natural, desolate appearance it presented was but a too faithful type, our traveller related to her husband all she had seen and heard, and (having earnestly prayed for guidance) asked what he thought respecting the desirableness of making further enquiries about so unpropitious a looking spot. He said, – 'Do as you like, do as you like!'

Thinking that a work *might* be done there for the glory of God, our heroine tried to find, through an agent, whether there might be a possibility of carrying her plans into effect. A person was consulted who had the property to dispose of. He strongly advised his applicant *not* to purchase Woodlands; for, the desolation of it was so great, that it would be impossible to build a house there, even with a view of making it an occasional residence, as neither man nor beast were scarcely ever seen about the place. He added, that no one would take the Manor, though it had been waiting for a purchaser for many, many years. All this seemed very unfavourable, but the praying enquirer felt that the greater the difficulty, the greater need there was for exertion and patient waiting; as, if this should be the place chosen by the Lord for work to be done therein, difficulties must be met with and overcome. A second and third visit was paid to Woodlands, and, finally, notwithstanding the urgent remonstrances of all who saw it, against the fixing upon so hopeless a task as trying to convert such a wilderness into a habitable place, it became the property of one who looked forward with assured but humble confidence to the being able to render it available for good, temporally and spiritually. Accordingly, workmen were employed; trees were felled, stones, ragged briars, etc., were removed from the choked-up vale; constant labour soon caused a clearance sufficient to commence the erection of a house. When the building was completed, grounds were laid out, and, in course of time, Woodlands Manor became the beautiful place it is now.

Let it not be supposed that the originator of this plan was contented with having secured a place of temporary residence 'just after her own heart!' Earnest prayer was continually made that it might become a repository of good, from which every soul in the surrounding, though distant hamlets, might hear not only of God, but of His love to a guilty world, in sending His beloved Son to die for sinners, that 'whosoever believeth in Him should not perish, but have everlasting life'. This was the grand object she had in view.

When a portion of the land was being dug, immediately behind the house now erected, many human skulls and bones were found; skeletons quite perfect, also pottery of very ancient fabricature, such as pieces of vases, jugs, etc., and what appeared to have formed a part of the ornament of a church. No one knew whether there had ever existed any living being, or that any building had been situated in this secluded valley; but, from the discoveries alluded to of human skeletons, and of various specimens of articles used by man, it was evident that people had lived, and that a church had formerly stood, there. A golden ring also was discovered in which a jewel was set; those who examined it pronounced it to be very, very ancient. Histories and documents were searched, from which was obtained distinct evidence that there had formerly existed a parish and a church at Woodlands. In the 15th year of Queen Elizabeth's reign, the remains of the decayed ruins of Woodlands Church were to be seen; at which time, the district was united to Wrotham as to its ecclesiastical jurisdiction; the rector of which, and the vicar of Kemsing, had a right to possess all the emoluments arising from it, 'till another church should be built'.

Centuries had rolled on and Woodlands was forgotten! No one dreamed of building a Church at desolate Woodlands! No attempt had been made to do anything to improve this forlorn, forsaken district.

But, the time had arrived when an important step was about to be taken by one whose *first* desire was to be an instrument in the Lord's hands of bringing poor, benighted souls to Christ. Prayer and faith were the first grand means used.

No effort was spared to secure the accomplishment of the object desired; and, as the Lord uses, sometimes, the weakest instruments to carry out His purposes, this humble labourer felt renewed vigour given to her, whilst endeavouring to satisfy the warmest desire of her heart – that of building a house of God in the place where His name was not known, to which souls might be drawn to hear the everlasting gospel preached. Earnest and continual prayer was put up to Him who, alone, could enable her to execute that for which she so ardently longed.

Money was required – all she could supply was given liberally and with a joyful heart; still, notwithstanding her large donations, all she wished could not be effected; the work could not be completed. No time was to be lost. Applications were made to such as are thankful to help forward any good work. It need not be mentioned that every such application was accompanied with prayer. There being no surrounding population to whom she could appeal for assistance, friends at a distance were called upon to cast their gifts into *this* treasury.

The hearts of many Christians were opened to give help to this labour of love. Sums came in abundantly; and the projectress of this object could not but see how wonderfully her prayers were, so far, answered, and that her work was owned by Him who put it into her heart to build a house for His name. Every stone, so to speak, in the building, was laid with prayer by her who longed to see 'living stones' worshipping in that sanctuary. Day by day the work progressed, and, at length, a most picturesque church was completed, near the manor house.

Great opposition had been made to the undertaking by many who thought it 'madness' to make the attempt! The more she was thwarted the higher did the prayer-offerer rise above the difficulties she met with – feeling that the greater the difficulty, the greater was the necessity to work; knowing that 'with God *all* things are possible' – and she was able exultingly to exclaim to all of them, when the work was finished, as she pointed to the answer to believing in prayer, 'What hath God wrought!' The late beloved Archbishop Sumner came down to Woodlands to consecrate the church. How did that heart beat with grateful delight, when, as the holy man led its possessor towards the edifice, he expressed to her his great satisfaction, and desired a large blessing upon all that had been done. Crowds were assembled from all parts of the county. What a strange sight in the lately unknown spot of Woodlands Manor!

The next thing, was to get an endowment for the church. That was also granted to her; and a faithful minister of the gospel was soon heard from its pulpit. When it became known that people could attend a place of worship within two or three miles from their homes, many came from the scattered hamlets, and also from the nearest villages. So that in this place – where it had been continually said to her (by those who disapproved of the attempt), 'What is the use of your building a church when there is nobody to come to it?' – a congregation was collected to overflowing, in the beautiful little church of Woodlands.

Having experienced the prospering hand of God in her undertaking, the projectress of it determined to build a school close to the church, hoping to draw the children from the distant farms and neighbouring parishes. This, also, she effected; and the prettiest of school-buildings may now be seen situated between the church and the manor house, in which a goodly number assemble to be taught the Word of God, and salvation through Jesus Christ our Lord.

The first thing which strikes the eye of a stranger upon entering the church yard, is a tombstone, upon which is graven the account of one 'who had humbly looked to Jesus for the pardon of her sins', ending with, 'For as in Adam all die, even so in Christ shall all be made alive'. 1 Cor.xv.22. It is a very impressive sight, under such circumstances; the gospel preached (as it were by a gone-one) even before entering the sanctuary; that same spot having previously been one of heathen darkness!

One more addition was wanting – a residence for the minister. Accordingly, a desirable spot was selected, on the slightly rising ground behind the manor house, where a parsonage has been erected corresponding with the church and school; which, with its surrounding gardens, fields, etc., seems to possess all that heart could wish, as regards *this* world; in fact it is impossible to imagine a prettier picture than that presented to one viewing the church, the school, the manor house, and the parsonage, from one of the heights of Woodlands Manor.

This little sketch is intended to exhibit the faithfulness of Him who has said 'If ye shall ask anything in My name, I will do it', and as an encouragement to the children of God to 'continue in prayer', however discouraging appearances may be, waiting patiently for the answer to it; which will assuredly come in His own good time, knowing that 'He is faithful who hath *promised*'.

Notes

Life on the North Downs

1   In 1829 Samuel Palmer made a drawing of 'The Bridge at Shoreham', showing a house upstream in the distance. The inscription reads, 'The Groombridges' house over the pollards'. This Mr Groombridge was a farmer.

2   Jack was an excellent storyteller but we both noticed how some of his stories had an anti-climactic ending. Just when you are expecting a dramatic conclusion, everything is suddenly resolved. This tendency is observed in other stories.

3   Dunstall Priory, Lord Dunsany's home, was built in the early 19th century on land that had belonged to the Prior of Charterhouse, London, in the 14th century. It was never itself a priory.

4   As mentioned in the background piece, Maplescombe is thought to be an 11th-century church abandoned in the 16th century. It was built from local flints, plastered inside and out, and enough of its walls survive for its plan to still be seen. It was a single-celled church with a semi-circular eastern apse. The burial ground has long been taken into cultivation.

5   *Pig and Whistle*. The name actually derives from 'piggen wassail' meaning bowl and wassail. A piggen was a bowl, the wassail, from Old Norse *ves heill* (good health), a drink to one's health. The locals would have come up with their twist on the name because of the smuggling connection. Samuel Palmer, the artist who lived in Shoreham from 1827-35 mentions the *Pig and Whistle* in his letters. He refers to Magpie Bottom as 'Pig and Whistle Bottom'.

6   Benjamin Harrison's son, Sir Edward Harrison, gives this description of Woodlands:

> Hidden in the hills at the upper end of a dry and deep chalk valley that runs into the Downs from Farningham is a hamlet called Woodlands. It contains little more than a large farm house, a tiny church and the vicarage. And beyond these, rolling open downs covered with turf and sprinkled with the daintiest chalk flowers. The beauty and seclusion of Woodlands could not but appeal to a man of Harrison's temperament.

Sir Edward Harrison, *Harrison of Ightham* (1928), p.51.

7   This was reminiscent of Sam dancing as described by Ronald Blythe in *Akenfield* (1969):

> The landlord holds up a large white hand as though he is going to give a blessing, but it falls on the light-switch panel. Sam stands up, buttoning his jacket, emptying his glass. He could be leaving – even when he reaches the bare floor he could be on his way home. But he stops, stretches like a wiry old cat, makes himself tall – and dances. His eyes blaze in the firelight. Huge polished boots fly. The dance is a kind of kicking stamp, coltish, vigorous. Sam's heel-irons actually produce sparks and this makes everybody

laugh. He dances and dances, eventually clasping his hands nonchalantly behind his back with a gesture of, 'Stop me when you've had enough ...' Nobody does and he has to stop himself, which happens in the midst of a crescendo of stamping. His body resumes its old slightly bent position gratefully and heaves with breath. The applause is solemn, a patter of clapping – no shouts. Young Hickey then opens his melodeon with a great yawning chord and Sam sings his song, with difficulty at first because he hasn't got his puff back, then with surprising strength. Like his dance, Sam's song is violent, full of attack. Nobody joins in though 'several' know the words backwards.

8   See background. The Romney family are recorded as farming land in this area from 1414.

Background to the Area

1   Sir Edward Harrison, *Harrison of Ightham* (1928), p.201.
2   *Textus Ruffensis*, a collection of early Rochester church documents which contains an 11th-century list of churches. Maplescombe and Woodlands are recorded as paying the full church rate (not chapel) for chrism oil used in baptism.
3   Zena Bamping, *West Kingsdown* (1991), p.40.
4   Dennis Clarke, translation of an Otford Custumal, 1284, Canterbury Cathedral MSE 24; Clarke and Stoyel, *Otford in Kent* (1975), p.265; White and Saynor, *Shoreham, A Village in Kent* (1989), p.245.
5   Edward Hasted, *The History and Topographical Survey of the County of Kent* (reprint, 1972), vol. III p.29.
6   Zena Bamping, *West Kingsdown* (1991), p.153.
7   White and Saynor, *Shoreham, A Village in Kent* (1989), p.170.
8   Zena Bamping, *West Kingsdown* (1991), p.40.

Bibliography

Bamping, Zena, *West Kingsdown, The Story of Three Villages in Kent* (1991)

Blythe, Ronald, *Akenfield, Portrait of an English Village* (1969)

Bowden, V.E., *The Story of Kemsing in Kent* (1994)

Brandon, Peter, *The North Downs* (2005)

Clarke, Dennis and Stoyel, Anthony, *Otford in Kent, a History* (1975)

Harrison, Sir Edward, *Harrison of Ightham* (1928)

Hasted, Edward, *The History and Topographical Survey of the County of Kent* (1972)

Jarrett, Philip, *Another Icarus: Percy Pilcher and the Quest for Flight* (1987)

White, Malcolm and Saynor, Joy, *Shoreham, A Village in Kent* (1989)

Index

Numbers in **bold** refer to illustration page numbers